And a Seed was Planted

Volume 2
Inclusion projects and learning experiences

And a Seed was Planted

Volume 2
Inclusion projects and learning experiences

Edited by
Sarah Kantartzis
Nick Pollard
Hanneke van Bruggen

Forewords by
Sridhar Venkatapuram
and
Elizabeth Townsend

w&b

MMXXI

ISBN 9781861776051 (this volume)
Set ISBN 9781861776242

Contents

Contents

Acknowledgements

We would like to thank all the contributors and the people who have worked with them, and with us, to make 'And a seed was planted...' possible. Putting together such a diverse collection of material translated from so many languages and with authors in locations across the world is always challenging, and always worthwhile. Two of our contributors, Linda Wilson and Ellen Ferguson, did not live to see their work published, and we would like to dedicate this project to their memories. There are lots of ways in which we have had help and contributions from our colleagues, friends and families from coffee and a bit of space to work in, to advice, for which we are grateful. We would especially like to thank everyone for persevering with us to publication.

Nick: I would like to thank Linda, Molly, Joshua, Daisy and Olivia for their patience and toleration during this project, including some unusual 'holidays', to facilitate meetings. Thanks also to the Occupational Therapy, Vocational Rehabilitation and Dietetics team and students at Sheffield Hallam University (past and present) for their continued support and interest in this work.

Sarah: Thank you to Christos, Katerina and Harry for your patience and understanding, and to our grandchildren, Lucas and Francesca, that arrived during this project and who give so much love and never ending joy! Thank you also to colleagues at Queen Margaret University Edinburgh for your continual support.

Hanneke: Thank you Sarah and Nick for working together and taking the long road together with all the contributors to the end of this project. Thanks also to Hotze, who patiently listened to me and continued to support. Thanks to my daughters, Mieke, Floortje and Sanne, who still tolerate that their mother is sometimes "absent" because she "has to" work.

Manifesto for occupation

Hanneke van Bruggen, Nick Pollard, Sarah Kantartzis

Health through occupation

Occupational therapy is about enabling people to do activities that are necessary and important to them and through these to participate in the society of which they are part. 'Occupation' means anything a person *does*. The significance of doing is often overlooked because it is so fundamental to human existence. All our human stories are accounts of things we have done, to become who we are, and the expression of our belonging in a world with others. Through our doing we have constructed, and continue to reconstruct what we do, where, when, how, why and with whom. Occupation, or simply 'doing', is something common to all people everywhere, at all stages of life. It is important not only for what each of us can do in our lifetimes, but also for the kind of world we are building for the future.

There is a fundamental relationship between health and occupation. Through our occupations we are able to orchestrate our lives in ways that enable us not only to survive, but also to develop our potential and express our skills, while creating and maintaining our connections with others. Through our occupation we can develop and maintain our families, neighbourhoods and communities as sources of belonging, opportunities and common action. Occupation therefore is not only important to each individual, but also, through our collective occupation we develop the kind of lives that we live together. Occupation is an essential factor in life quality, and in the experience of being human.

However, occupation does not always lead to such positive and health supporting outcomes, and there are many challenges to meaningful and purposeful occupation for some people. These include disability; illness, trauma and disease; differences in access to food, water, shelter, transport, utilities; relative poverty; differences in social status and citizenship rights; differences in legal status; the economic and social consequences of war and other forms of conflict, climate and climate change; pollution; the planning and development of built structures; the effects of social change arising from shifts in population such as ageing, migration or resulting from disease such as HIV/AIDS; the consequences of disaster; personal tragedy; poor government; economic restructuring. The list is not comprehensive, and the factors can be combined in multiple forms with localised and specific effects.

Our concern is that the link between occupation and health has been consistently overlooked. In occupational therapy there has been an ongoing focus on the impact of illness, disease and trauma on the individual. There has been less attention paid to the social determinants of health and to the impact of social exclusion. Health promoting occupation is a key element in public health and in preventing ill-health. Overlooking this has restricted working with the potential of occupation to express and support human flourishing and develop healthy communities.

We argue that the expression of human health is more than an index of outcomes or therapeutic interventions. We support a view of health as not a stable and normative concept but as unbounded and potentially ever extending, incorporating notions of people's flourishing, the ongoing satisfaction of needs and the development of their potentials as fully included members of the society in which they live. We are calling for a discussion about the value and importance of occupation, not just for occupational therapists alone, but for everyone in health and social care and human sciences. We are calling for a rethink of the way health outcomes relate to personal and collective experiences and human values which are based in the understanding of doing. We need to work with others in reclaiming the value of occupation for all and as an important part of public health.

We are also concerned that the idea of occupation is bigger than can be realised through the profession of occupational therapy. Access to health promoting occupations can be a goal for social changes. These occupations have the potential to be owned by everyone, as they are concerned with how we live together and can be based in shared experiences. However, the knowledge and experience that is common to all is not always valued simply because of its common ownership, so there is a role for some people to critically explore ways to make this value more evident. Again, this should engage both those who are occupational therapists and people who are willing to work with them. The future of evidence for the transformative power of occupation is through co-production, participant action, and the sharing of the discussions about it with others.

A call for change

In order to promote health through occupation we need to work to address the multiple factors that influence people's possibility to engage in health promoting occupation. We need to work together to move forward, to create opportunities for all, to achieve individual and societal flourishing. We need to work in partnership, across sectors, disciplines, political and social divides to create the conditions for change in our education, practice and research. To do this we must:

- Build and maintain active dialogues, and negotiate alliances and strategies with disadvantaged and excluded groups and individuals, disability groups and carers' organisations, practitioners and researchers.
- Effectively campaign for health promoting occupation including participation rights across all levels of disability and social barriers
- Develop different forms of action from protest to social enterprises which exemplify and are underpinned by health-promoting occupation
- Challenge the acceptance of social and the resulting health inequalities, through occupation-based practices and particularly those that incorporate sustainable and inclusive economic growth

Call for contributors

This call for change requires multiple partnerships with many and diverse actions. In considering our own potential contribution to this process we consider that it may be useful to develop a book that will provide both theoretical discussions but also discussion of practical and specific projects and actions. We intend that the book will set out examples of practice, narratives, research and theory which explore, explain and promote the connection between occupation-based practices, social inclusion and health. Our intention is to solicit contributions from a wide range of stakeholders, individuals and chapter-writing teams, including: lay persons, service users, administrators, students, professionals, building a 'tapestry' of experiences and ideas that is not only a textbook but a manual for practice, accessible to all. It will address:

- Understanding the importance of occupation in people's lives and its links with the social determinants of health, public health and prevention.
- Why occupation based practice and occupational therapists? Towards a wider awareness of occupation, and making sense of what occupational therapists might offer community groups.
- How occupation based practice fits in wider perspectives of social inclusion work
- Moving from occupational therapy practice based around individuals to occupation based practice with groups and communities
- The particular characteristics of occupation based practice, including:
- Identifying significant variations with occupational therapy practice in traditional settings, including professional boundaries, compartmentalization of responsibilities and being a community member;
- Recognising change – critical moments and turning points;
- Managing risks and dependency;
- Professionalism and power with vulnerable people as colleagues;
- Managing delegation and responsibility for sustainability;
- Common sense, tacit knowledge and articulating occupation;
- Project and change management, progress and timescales
- Strategies for identifying outcomes for funders, partners and managers;

Thank you

Foreword

The argument that the purpose of politics and the polity is to enable citizens to pursue flourishing lives is most often linked to Aristotle, the ancient Greek philosopher (330 BCE). Centuries of discussions and debates have taken place and still continue regarding various aspects of this argument such as what is a flourishing life, who is included as a citizen, what are the boundaries of politics, what are good processes for governing a polity, and so forth. There has also been much discussion about whether this argument can be reconciled with various religions, including Christianity, as well as the possibility of such an argument in other societal political traditions. For example, tall pillars erected during the reign of the first Buddhist emperor Ashoka (220 BCE) identify various entitlements of citizens and instructions for living a good life.

While it may not be apparent to people outside, academic political philosophy in the Anglo-American world has been thriving over the past few decades because various philosophers have revived the direct conversation with Aristotle and Ashoka by putting forward what they argue to be theories of a good and just society for the modern world. In some cases, individuals have put forward a theory of a just world, or global justice. The person often credited with instigating this activity is John Rawls (1921-2002). In 1971, in his book, *A Theory of Justice*, he laid out critiques of various secular approaches to a good society and then put forward a careful argument for the purpose of some basic social institutions, what citizens are entitled to, how they should engage with each other in mutual cooperation, and so forth.

One of the curious and frustrating things about Rawls's stupendous effort is that he did not give sufficient consideration to health. The state of one's physical and mental functioning directly affects what one can be and do on any given day as well as what plans one can make and the life one can pursue. So how can something so important not be included in the consideration of what public institutions are meant to do, and how fellow members of society should treat each other? One plausible explanation is that Rawls, like many other individuals, particularly in the United States, believed that health is a 'natural good.' Health is seen as something that luck /nature gives to some people or takes away. Health is also something that individuals control through their personal behaviours. And, society addresses poor health through provision of sufficient income to individuals that will allow the purchase of adequate 'healthcare' to return them back to normal functioning. And, without going into much detail, Rawls thought that people who are born severely impaired or who will never return to 'normal' should be dealt with by charitable institutions – not our justice promoting institutions. Given his quite monumental project to articulate a theory of a just and well-ordered society, he was focused on the 'typical' or 'ideal' individual that is able bodied and interested in pursuing a flourishing life. Similarly, he wanted to focus on one society before thinking about a world with many societies, some of which may not even share some of the basic tenets of his just society.

Rawls's theory has received enormous scrutiny resulting in both criticism and praise. Nevertheless, across the discipline and world over, he is credited with bringing back our philosophical attention to the idea of social and global justice, or the question of a good society. Other philosophers have responded to Rawls, and all theories previous to his, by offering their own alternatives. They all start from the point that all human beings are morally equal and value freedom. And from here, different theories focus on what individuals are entitled to from their social environments including public institutions as well as how people should treat each other. Now, while this has been going on in academic literature, it is not hard to see that the same questions are in play in 'real world' politics across the world. Who is included in a society? What are they entitled to? Which institutions are required and which are not? What makes a good institution? How should citizens treat each other?

It is against this background that it is profoundly exciting to see Occupational Science seeking to identify its moral or ethical mission. One could situate Occupational Science as part of health institutions that constitute basic social institutions. That is, Occupational Science is part of a basic social institution whose primary purpose is social justice, or enabling individuals to pursue flourishing lives. Or, more courageously, Occupational Science could aim to stand on its own and assert that it seeks to enable flourishing lives everywhere—within and outside health institutions. Nevertheless, in either case, linking a science to a moral mission requires rigorous and careful reasoning that cuts across the sciences and humanities. And importantly, it requires a clear engagement with a conception or theory of social justice, or a good society. The present volume reflects the kind of deep empirical engagement and mutual reflection between Occupational Science and social justice philosophy we need right now.

I personally feel enormous pride and delight that Occupational Science academics and practitioners have found something helpful in my argument for health justice, and the capabilities approach more generally. While I invite and look forward to further engagement, I also want to encourage a much wider engagement with all the other philosophical approaches to social and global justice. The idea that there is a group of people who believe in and aim to help individuals, particularly those that are marginalized in a society, to be and do things in their lives that they value, should be more widely known and appreciated. Philosophers will benefit from knowing that it is not just a theoretical argument, but embodied in the work of Occupational Science practitioners. And Occupational Science will likely benefit from seeing all the variety of conceptions of justice and how philosophers reason and justify arguments for equity. The present volume represents the start of such an engagement, and I hope, will initiate a new phase in both Occupational Science and in our broader reasoning about social and global justice.

Sridhar Venkatapuram
London

Foreword

What an accomplishment! With *And a Seed was Planted* the European editors and a global array of authors have created a unique book about transforming societies day by day. Here is a book full of ideas and examples for globally minded persons who are committed to engagement 'with' versus doing 'to' others in promoting health, well-being, and justice around the world.

And a Seed was Planted offers a collection of very interesting approaches to complex, global issues based on citizen participation, not relying on top down governmental action. The projects are socially minded with awareness that policies, economics, rituals, and other social structures are at the root of social exclusion, inequity, poverty, and other conditions that persists to this day across parts of Europe, Asia, Africa, South, and North America. It's interesting to consider that some readers may find the approaches described here as ordinary because they are based on engaging people in day-to-day occupations like gardening and employment. Yet these are radical approaches because they challenge the status quo for marginalized or vulnerable groups, like the persons with visual impairments or refugees, whose participation in daily life is restricted beyond their individual conditions. Transformation is of concern here particularly in times and places where disabled people and others face restricted participation, including their lack of voice and choice in health and social services.

This book should attract any practitioner who engages participants in projects with aims for transforming societies anywhere in the world. Hopefully occupational therapists will be especially pleased to see projects that, to me, illustrate the untapped potential of this profession to create an occupationally just world. In seeing occupational therapy's potential with the examples and projects in this book, readers may imagine new ways to link day-by-day life with health, well-being, and daily life.

As an occupational therapist with 50 years experience, I celebrate the book's reclamation of engagement in occupation – action beyond talking – and the commitment to practices that illustrate funding and approaches outside as well as inside medical systems. Despite global job pressures, from salaries and job descriptions to standardized protocols and evidence-based practice based on individualistic, biomedical priorities, the authors present an array of ways in which occupational therapists can break away. Community occupational therapy, government policy-based occupational therapy, justice-oriented occupational therapy, occupational therapy leadership, and related ideas are all championed and legitimized through the authors' stories.

Why am I so enthusiastic? Clearly I love the ideas and practice examples in *And a Seed was Planted*. I also love the accessibility of these in seven clearly organized sections. Section 1 nicely introduces Social Inclusion, Occupation, and Occupation-Based Social Inclusion, plus a story by an artist with a difficult life. The book is more than a collection of practice stories with Section II illuminating *Theoretical Views* related to projects, and Section III on projects that profile *Shifting Perspectives*. Section IV (*Learning Inclusion*) and Section V (*Projects*) together include 12 chapters of wonderful examples of occupation-based social inclusion practices. Beyond the neatness of the book's structure, I also love *Occupation-Based Social Inclusion* because the projects illustrate the intent of the 1948 Declaration of Human Rights (United Nations) with its naming of education, housing, employment, and other everyday sites for doing human rights and justice. Amartya Sen (2009) might see the projects described here as real life ways to reduce what he called 'inclusionary incoherence', referring to gaps between ideas like justice, and everyday realities.

Finally, congratulations are due to the team that made *Occupation-Based Social Inclusion* possible. After what must have been many hours of collaboration, translation, and editing, the editors and authors can be proud of their invaluable gift to the English-reading world. With their efforts, English-readers are privileged to learn about innovative approaches to occupation-based social inclusion around the world.

Elizabeth Townsend, PhD, OTRegPEI, FCAOT
Professor Emerita, Dalhousie University
Liz.Townsend@Dal.ca
Adjunct Professor, University of Prince Edward Island
etownsend@upei.ca

Prologue to Volume 2
Learning inclusion and projects

Occupational therapy originated in social reform, but early in its history became allied with medicine, a biomedical perspective and a focus on individual health. Over the last two decades the profession has recognised the value of the work of its pioneers and argued for principles such as occupational justice and the right to health-promoting occupations, social inclusion, and for forms of involvement based in the community which centre around people doing things together for social change. In *'And a seed was planted...' Occupation based approaches for social inclusion* the Editors have set out to show how these ideas are being put into practice internationally.

This is the second volume of a three-volume set. The first volume opened with three chapters in which the Editors offer an introduction to the main concepts discussed throughout the set – social inclusion, occupation, and approaches to occupation-based social inclusion. A further two sections offered chapters on Theoretical Views and Shifting Perspectives.

This second volume takes forward these ideas in two sections, Learning Inclusion and Projects. In the first section contributors from Europe, India and the United States explore occupation-based learning experiences in diverse settings, both as part of formal education as well as learning through living together. The second section presents accounts of community-based projects located in various countries of Europe and Asia, illustrating the influences of health and social systems, cultural norms and expectations. The projects presented are at different stages of development thereby offering insights into the various stages in the life of a project, including planning and building partnerships.

About the authors

Varvara Apostologlou, ELSiTO member

Frank Auracher, Gemeinwesenarbeit, Quartiersmanagement und Präventionsstrategie CTC, Stadtteilbüro Nordstadt, Lebenshilfe e.V. Hildesheim, Germany

Dr Katrina Bannigan, BD, BSc, PhD, MRCOT, SFHEA, School of Health and Life Sciences, Glasgow Caledonian University, UK

Pamela Block, Ph.D. Professor, Department of Anthropology, Faculty of Social Science, Western University, London, Ontario, Canada

Katrin Bode, Ev. Martin-Luther-Kirchengemeinde Hildesheim Nordstadt-Drispenstedt, Hildesheim, Germany

Theodoros Bogeas, ELSiTO member

Hanneke E. van Bruggen, Hon. Dscie, Bsc OT, FWFOT, Director of Facilitation and Participation of Disadvantaged Groups (FAPADAG), The Netherlands, Senior Lecturer Ivane Javakhishvili Tbilisi State University (TSU), Georgia, Adjunct Prof. Dalhousie University, Canada, Honorary Research Fellow in the school of Health Sciences in the University of Kwazulu-Natal, South Africa

Hans-Jürgen Buttlar, Ev. Martin-Luther-Kirchengemeinde Hildesheim Nordstadt-Drispenstedt, Hildesheim, Germany

Viviane Constabel, BSc, Former student at HAWK University of Applied Sciences and Arts Hildesheim/Holzminden/Göttingen, Germany

Miranda Cunningham, Lecturer in Occupational Therapy, University of Plymouth, UK

Kazunari Daigo, Vice chairman, Non-profit Organization Laule'a. Formerly working at Medical Corporation Meiho-kai Shin Totsuka Hospital, Japan

Abelardo Apollo I. David, Jr., MOccThy, OTRP, Rehabilitation and Empowerment of Adults and Children with Handicap Foundation, Inc., Independent Living Learning Learning Centre, Inc., Academia Progresiva de Manila, Inc., University of Sto. Tomas, Philippines

Susie Dent, Co-manager of Students and Refugees Together (START), UK

Dr Patricia Eyres, BSc, MSc, PhD, FEHA, MRCOT Associate Lecturer in Occupational Therapy, University of Plymouth, UK

Fiona Fraser, BSc, MSc, FHEA, MRCOT Lecturer in Occupational Therapy, University of Plymouth, UK

Yasuaki Hayama, Representative, Care Planets Co., Ltd: http://www.careplanets. co.jp. Vice chairman, NPO "Manabiai" Learning Together https://manabiai.org/ manabiai-learning-together. Japan

Brigitta Hemmelmeier-Händel, Landscape architect, Graduate engineer at Lebensorte - engineering offices for open space planning and landscape architecture. Austria

Margaret Jelley, (Retired) social work lecturer, University of Plymouth, UK

Sarah Kantartzis, ELSiTO member, Senior lecturer in occupational therapy in the Division of Occupational Therapy and Arts Therapies at Queen Margaret University, Edinburgh, UK

Maria Karampetsou, ELSiTO member

Pamela Karp, EdD,OTR/L, CHT, New York Institute of Technology, USA

Ursula Koselleck, Ev. Martin-Luther-Kirchengemeinde Hildesheim Nordstadt-Drispenstedt, Hildesheim, Germany

Stefanos Lazopoulos, ELSiTO member

Carla Liebig, BSc, Former student at HAWK University of Applied Sciences and Arts Hildesheim/Holzminden/Göttingen, Germany

Jacqueline Mckenna, Senior Lecturer and Programme Leader for Occupational Therapy (PT Route) and MSc Geriatric Medicine at University of Salford, Salford, UK

Marina Malfa, ELSiTO member

Miyuki Minato. Former professor of Kibi International University. Ibaraki Prefectural University of Health Sciences Lecturer (part time)

Hajime Morishima, Chief Operating Officer, MEDICAL CORPORATION OLIVE. Formerly working at Saitama National Hospital, Japan

Susanne Mulzheim, Occupational therapist, MSc in Health Promotion. Austria

Panagiotis Papantoniou, ELSiTO member

Nick Pollard, Senior lecturer in occupational therapy at Sheffield Hallam University, UK

Steven Roberts, Freelance Conductor and member of the Association of British Choral Directors, the Musicians' Union, Life member of the Royal Philharmonic Society, adjudicator member of The British and International Federation of Festivals, Conductor and Musical Director of Altrincham Choral Society, Chesterfield Philharmonic Choir and Honley Male Voice Choir.

Maria Roussi, ELSiTO member

Dr. Sandra Schiller, HAWK University of Applied Sciences and Arts Hildesheim/ Holzminden/Göttingen, Germany

John Shanth Kumar Joseph, Managing Trustee of YEAH (Youth Empowered in Action for Humanity), Bangalore, India.

Salvador Simó Algado. Adjunct Director Mental Health Chair, Mental Health and Social Innovation Research group, UVic-UC. Spain

Anita Slade, Centre for Patient Reported Outcome Research, Institute of Applied Health, University of Birmingham, UK

Marnie Smith, Lecturer in Occupational Therapy, University of Plymouth, UK

Ellen Tickle

Vasiliki Tsonou, ELSiTO member

Dr Rebecca Twinley, School of Health Sciences, University of Brighton, UK

Lyn Westcott, Professional Lead Consultant Occupational Therapy, University of Hertfordshire, UK

Hiromi Yoshikawa. Assisted with translation. Hiroshima Prefectural University, Department of Occupational Therapy. Japan

Section 4
Learning inclusion

This section includes a diverse range of learning experiences, from within formal learning environments to the informal processes of living together, all aiming for change in how those engaged experience and understand the people and the society around them. Some demonstrate first steps and isolated approaches and it will be important to consider how these can be related to wider processes, for example to curriculum content as a whole, but also how approaches may be further developed and built upon.

This section opens with a narrative from the Greek members of the learning partnership ELSITO (Empowering Learning for Social Inclusion Through Occupation) sharing their reflections on the process of learning social inclusion together during the doing of everyday occupations.

Eyres et al's chapter then turns to the more formal learning environment of the Higher Education Institution and a bachelor programme in occupational therapy in the UK. Here the need for development of the programme is underpinned by the recognition of occupation as the core process of occupational therapy, and of occupational needs as the focus of the profession which may relate to marginalised groups. The shift in focus includes from the individual to the collective, from a bio-medical model of health to a more social model, and is explored in relation to enacting changes for students in their learning opportunities and experiences. An interdisciplinary project with a local, charitable organisation, Students and Refugees Together (START) is described as part of this process.

The following chapter by Schiller et al, from Hildesheim in Germany, moves firmly into a local community and an ongoing urban gardening project, which is bringing together community workers, a university teacher and occupational therapy students and a number of volunteers. The processes of incorporating the potential of the various partners, together with the power of occupation are explored.

Karp and Block, writing from the USA, describe a rather different experience for students in the following chapter when they are invited to participate in a Salamander Project workshop. This community artistic process encouraged the participants to critically explore their own prejudices and attitudes towards disability. The focus on an event rather than an ongoing project invites consideration of the multiple ways in which students educational experiences may be structured and nested within the overall frameworks of educational structures.

The following chapter, again focusing on higher education, by McKenna, Roberts and Tickle, takes a different perspective in exploring some of the structural issues around the processes of the development of occupational therapy curricula. Despite the institutional demands for greater service user involvement in the development of educational curricula in the UK, this chapter displays some of the complexities of this process.

Completing this section is a chapter by Shant and van Bruggen that discusses the mobilisation processes of an organisation located in India – YEAH – that is working as a capacity-based initiative with the youth of India to educate and empower them towards transformation. Working with the philosophies and educational ideas of Ambedkar, Freire and Dewey YEAH shifts education beyond traditional establishments and grounds it in shared processes of reflection, support, critique and action.

Chapter 1
Doing and learning together for social inclusion: The Greek ELSiTO group

Barbara Apostologlou, Stefanos Lazopoulos,
Theodoros Bogeas, Sarah Kantartzis, Vasiliki Tsonou,
Maria Karampetsou, Panagiotis Papantoniou,
Marina Malfa, and Maria Roussi

Introduction

ELSiTO (Empowering Learning for Social Inclusion through Occupation) was initially established in 2009 as a European collaboration to explore the nature and processes of social inclusion, in partnership with persons from vulnerable social groups (particularly persons experiencing mental health problems). The group members included service users, occupational therapists (lecturers, professionals, students) and health professionals, all using the title of 'ELSiTO member'. The aims of the partnership were to explore good practices in projects promoting social inclusion and to develop our community projects in collaboration, enhancing social inclusion at multiple levels through economic, social, cultural occupation and by enhancing members' competences and collaborative learning strategies (Ammeraal et al., 2011). The means for accomplishing this was the experience of learning about social inclusion together[1] (ELSiTO, 2015).

Funded by the Grundtvig Lifelong Learning Programme of the European Union for two years (2009 - 2011), ELSiTO organised four international visits, produced a booklet and a website (www.elsito.net). The group presented at international congresses, gave public seminars in Athens, Greece, and a workshop for occupational therapy students of the University of Brussels, Belgium. Further collaborative accounts of the group have been published[2] (Nikaki & Bogeas, 2010; Kantartzis et al., 2012; Ammeraal et al., 2013).

The goal of this chapter is not to summarise the existing theory on social inclusion nor to present the outcomes of the partnership, which can be found on the ELSiTO website (www.elsito.net), but to share our reflections on our experiences of learning about social inclusion. The authors represent the Greek members of ELSiTO. To write this chapter, two members agreed to lead the process and all members participated twice in conversations during our monthly meetings with the following themes:

- What and how do we learn in ELSiTO.
- Sharing an experience from our participation in the group.

The chapter leaders kept notes and recorded these conversations. In this chapter, the term 'he' will be used to refer to any ELSiTO member, regardless of their gender and the term 'we' will be used to refer to the Greek ELSiTO members as a group, unless otherwise specified.

How it works

The group was initially created by Sarah Kantartzis who, together with several occupational therapists, approached day centres for persons with experience of mental illness and a social club for the elderly to advertise the group and to invite people to join. One person brought another, and after a year there were more than 10 members. After the completion of the initial funded programme the Greek ELSiTO group remains open to anyone who is interested in social inclusion. Members include service users, family members, occupational therapists (educators, practitioners and students) and other professionals, such as nurses. The group meets regularly every second Sunday of the month. New members continue to join, prompted by word of mouth. The group is supported by the Hellenic Association of Occupational Therapists (HAOT) by being the named partner for the Grundtvig grant, using its quarters for the meetings, and by promoting ELSiTO to its members. After coming to a few meetings, if new members decide that they want to participate, they fill out an application form to HAOT at no cost.

When the original funding ended, there were several reasons why members chose to continue the group: the need to not end our collaboration abruptly; the special meaning that the group had for each member individually; and the need for us to continue experiencing social inclusion in the unique way which has been established by ELSiTO. Members wanted to empower each other to develop the competences for participation in social inclusion processes. They also wanted to disseminate and share the group's ideas with other people in Greece.

Through ELSiTO, we learn to co-exist and walk together in the here and now of each meeting, through the occupation (activity) in which we choose to engage. We replenish ourselves with life experiences, either by going to new places that we wouldn't have gone alone or playing a game which we hadn't ever imagined ourselves playing, being free to express our emotions, our thoughts and our interest for others. Equity, respect for the differences and for the uniqueness of each other characterise the group and its meetings. Any ground rules or processes have arisen and are used during our quest for knowledge of social inclusion through the active participation of the members.

The mode of group operation is as follows:

- In every meeting we keep minutes and we plan what will take place in the next meeting. At the beginning we like to set our agenda and discuss these subjects. We also like sharing our news. Many times it is important to re-orientate ourselves to the group's purposes and to reflect on its good operation.
- Members communicate and interact between meetings through emails. Messages include suggestions about the place we will meet each time, and we run e-voting

to take decisions regarding the place we will meet and the activity we will do. This is based on the majority's choice, and it is an act which is based on direct democracy as interpreted in Ancient Greece.

- The choice of meeting place reflects the different energies or moods of the group. There are times when we feel extrovert and so we choose a park for a picnic or try something new. Alternatively, we choose a quiet place indoors when we feel that we have serious subjects to discuss, such as writing a book chapter. In the following parts of this chapter and through our narratives, this communication is evident and the richness it contains derives from the group meetings.

The creative evolution of the group

During discussions about this chapter we developed several questions regarding what we have learnt or what has changed in us. From its beginning ELSiTO has had a creative evolution through which the group has continued to operate, developing steadily as a living 'class'. This has been an attempt at a different type of connection or relationship between very different people, who wish however to feel and build together the notion or concept of inclusion. This kind of inclusion matters to all of us, it involves what we do together and what kind of relationships we have. The group represents experiential learning through occupations. This living class is not static within a classroom but is moving and is dynamic in terms of space, occupation and participants. It is a class in which there are no teachers and students, no one is the knowledge-keeper and no one is the non-knower. All together we start from the same point to learn about social inclusion and in this journey we use occupations as our vehicle.

We have called our group process creative evolution: it is a group which lives, evolves, and moves on and its members benefit through its shared lived experience. Diversity, co-existing and respect for each one's differences are important factors which enable the group to evolve.

Continuing our quest for social inclusion through experiential learning, our life in the Greek ELSiTO group has taught us the following:

- Be flexible and accept the unpredictable. For example, due to misunderstanding, instead of drinking coffee at a place called «Το Καφενείο των Μουσικών» (a traditional 'Musicians Kafenion'), we ended up eating supper at 5.00 p.m. (we usually eat after 8.00 p.m.), singing and dancing to folk tunes such as island songs (dancing in groups or in pairs with a quick rhythm), zeimpekiko (a slow dance performed by one person, with the rest creating a circle around him) or hasapiko (a slow group dance). A member stated that he really enjoyed this afternoon as he felt that the group would not be critical of his dancing, and he felt free to express himself.
- The importance of our self-organisation, arranging the meeting place each time, informing each other and generally through the operation mode of the group. As we participate and act in the group, we understand better the way we act in our personal life. A member says that through the responsibilities he takes on in the group (such as to call a member or bring a game or some fruit juice to the

meetings) he feels more included. We are wondering though, if it is only the responsibilities that he takes on that affect inclusion or is it the 'doing together' too. Even at those times when the group does something with which a member cannot engage, the member is free to share his difficulty or his lack of interest and find an alternative way of participating. For example, when we decided to play some group activities, some members were outside of the group and either they were giving instructions or just watched the games.

- The experience of inclusion and communication as well as how each of us feels in the group is something personal and definitely not the same for everyone. A member declares that within the group he finds the communication he misses from his daily life and that the group is constituted of ten people who speak the same 'essential language'. He also mentioned that he would always come together with an older member because he felt secure but that in the previous meeting he felt sufficiently confident to come alone.

- To respond to a challenge. One of the newest members says that, like all new things, inclusion in the group is a challenge, especially relating with members and the group as a whole: 'I don't miss having people around me. Each time I leave the group I wonder what my motivation is to be there and what it has to offer to me. I initially came because an older member suggested it; and when he was absent I missed him a lot. That was perhaps essential at the beginning. It is a challenge to see for yourself how much you can be included in a group. The most difficult paths are solitary but that does not exclude the others'. This member has come to recognise that being solitary is not necessarily about exclusion, or excluding others, and that inclusion involves missing those who are absent.

- It offers us space for reflection and self-analysis. Another member reports: 'nowadays, people cannot do many of the things that are in their interest because they feel other situations burden them and so they cannot do what they want. In the ELSiTO group members can leave their problems behind and they are occupied with the here and now, being spontaneous and authentic. From our birth and beyond, as we grow up we belong to groups. I don't think that we choose all the groups in which we are involved. But this group, ELSiTO, is something we choose. The emails I receive are a beautiful and pleasant surprise, because it is like getting news from friends who are part of my parea (companions or group of friends)'

- We like changes. By changing meeting points and activities we have a beautiful plurality.

- We learn through questioning, asking 'what is the ELSiTO group?' The group isn't about the need to drink a coffee, nor to do psychotherapy, but to accept each other as we are, share the roles and exchange them, such as making suggestions to the group, preparing the meeting, informing others, etc. Similarly, a small group (like ours) can be seen as a thumbnail portrait of society, in which we need to listen to each others' opinion, the way others face reality and their ideas of how the group should work, both what they expect and what are they willing to offer to the group.

- To be authentic through the group. A member writes in a note: 'I feel that we stand up for our co-existence, our equal and authentic relationships which fulfil us with beautiful emotions and unite us. As time passes by, our relationships strengthen, have more essence, become more beautiful, stronger, amazing and more and more and more…. We've learned to write and send 'positive energy through emails', showing care and interest'.

The first experiences of ELSiTO and the personal journey of each member within it

Each member has something to remember from the ELSiTO 'journey'. Here are some of our memories:

Building collaboration brick by brick. 'I remember somehow my first contact and how I felt strange being asked to participate in events when other members of ELSiTO had come from abroad and during the educational visits under the Grundtvig programme. I have a strong memory of trying to communicate with people who spoke a different language, with whom we had common interests and we wanted to organise the one-day seminar altogether. This is the biggest thing I have learnt, that when people collaborate something beautiful can be created brick by brick, with whatever strength and ability each has, by helping each other, one person seeing a solution where another has not. That is, after all, the moment I felt myself to have matured in the group. When I recognised that I would make it with the help and support of others and not just by myself.'

Organising the seminars. 'For me, of all the experiences we have lived through together, the most important were the organisation of the two one-day seminars. The significance was our equal and common participation as speakers and as members of ELSiTO in the presentations and workshops. It was an opportunity to participate without being divided into professionals and non-professionals. We demonstrated our 'Greek hospitality' and our ability as a group to organise international meetings perfectly! I find it important that we have created an authentic and equal relationship, which makes me feel that it is invaluable for us all!'

I participate as a co-citizen. 'One of the first meetings of the Greek group was held at the Areos Park (a central park in Athens). It was a place that I have never been to before and I remember that it was very hot, we hadn't brought a lot of water with us, we didn't find a place to sit easily and I began to feel responsible for the members and the group as a whole. We started playing some ball games (like volleyball) and I remember that some members played and some did not. We had a good time. However, it made me reflect on the responsibility that each one of us has for the group. As a health professional I was used to having an increased (as I saw it) responsibility; it didn't matter whether I wanted to play a game or not, but I 'should' play it with pleasure because it was part of my work. Now, I understand that ELSiTO needs something else; it needs me to participate as a citizen, to take care of the group as a whole and myself within and through the group. This demands a different attitude and perception from what I had as a professional, and I wonder how professionals can be citizens and professionals simultaneously?'

The recipe for happiness. 'I remember the time that we met in the café Svoura (taverna in the centre of Athens) and together we created the 'recipe for happiness'.

Our scripts were full of humanity, companionship and warmth and I was very happy that we had that afternoon together and shared these emotions. Afterwards, we discussed our personal goals (such as to stop smoking or participate in a vocational programme) and the group was trying to motivate each other to succeed with advice, smiles and ideas. That day was important for me for a further reason. At the end of our conversation a dispute arose and it was solved in the ideal way, in my opinion. Both members expressed directly and with honesty what they felt, it became clear that neither had intended to annoy the other, so they apologised and….that was it! I believe this example represents the quality of our relationships that we have developed, our competence to discuss and share different ideas and attitudes towards life and to solve any disputes.'

Equality of expression. 'I remember our meeting in Murtillo (a coffee shop that is run as a social enterprise by people from vulnerable groups/with special needs). I shared my thoughts about inviting our own people (family) to one of our meetings. A member suggested some words I was using [e.g. useful, purposeful, necessary] were inappropriate. Behind these words, I was thinking how fragile the group may be when it is confronted by possible 'dangers'. My anxiety was to protect what we had created all together. Her reaction helped me redefine my role in the group, as an equal member. She made me wonder if there is such a risk. Through her own actions (i.e. participating with her fiancé in the group), I reconsidered my thoughts, especially about being prepared for something new. It is helpful that we can express ourselves and our concerns freely and share our experiences. The group supports its members, even when they are in a difficulty or they disagree.'

Positive energy means a positive environment. 'After the first meeting of September in Rozalia (a restaurant in the centre of Athens), which was an introduction and a nice surprise, I would say that my motive for the continuation of my participation in the group was the positive energy that I received, the ability for expression, spontaneity and sensitiveness. This answers the question what does support mean inside the group. Regarding a recent question that one member asked through email – if the citizen and the professional could coexist – I answer yes, because we come to the group as a whole, as a personality, not only with the one characteristic or the other.

We create our own games. 'I remember the meeting when we decided to build a game of our own for ELSiTO! Our table was full of papers, colored markers and ideas. We were singing softly to one another, to try to explain in that way which song each of us was proposing for the game, while exchanging the markers over our heads. All this was taking place in a coffee shop where other people were peeping to see what we were up to! Except for having fun, it was a very special moment, as we all created a complete game together from scratch, which we tried to play later on. We had real motivation to cooperate with each other, driven by enjoyment, and having the feeling that everybody was participating equally in the group, not only in theory but also in practice'.

We create all together. 'I remember when I first heard about ELSiTO from Sarah and I went to the first meeting that was being held in BABEL (a day center for refugees *and immigrants in Athens). I was in the beginning of a new pursuit in relation to the personal meaning of my life and to something I like: to be a member of a group. I live inside groups, with groups from the groups, I love groups; to share, to listen, to participate, to create. For me, this creativity is the word that suits me best to describe the ELSiTO group. It is creative to be together with other people, to do things together, to cultivate relationships, to learn through others. In that first meeting I attended, while being lost like other people in the economic crisis, ELSiTO formed for me a way of opposing the crisis. I came to a neighborhood of immigrants, to a day centre for their children and I met a group of people who create together. That was it, and from that moment I wait eagerly for our next meeting'.*

Leadership

Leadership was a challenging role in the ELSiTO group. Equal participation for the leader was and is in contradiction to the usual position which a leader has, such as being the expert, decisive, auditing and guiding the group. Along with former personal experiences in group leading (that are simultaneously an asset and an obstacle), the role of leader transformed to coordinator, enabler and an equal member. The role came to include an overall care for the group and its processes. The leader/coordinator usually initiates mail discussion, reminds the date, the place for meeting, any arrangements that have been decided (who will bring what if necessary). Also, he usually coordinates discussion if necessary and initiates a discussion of the year's planning in September.

As explained above, leadership was acted initially in the traditional form, i.e. first members were added by the leader. The leader had been initially the only person responsible for the goals, the group processes and the coordination for the group which afterwards was transferred to all members. After funding, the Greek group used new tools within the group. Minutes were written by any member who would then send them by email until the next meeting. There is a group diary which includes the writings of the group during each meeting under a theme (such as 'The recipe for happiness' explained above), which is commonly decided at the moment. Another member is responsible to take the diary, forward the writings to all members through email and bring the diary to the next meeting.

The role of coordinator is continuing to change over time. The first coordinator moved abroad and another member became the coordinator gradually in a natural, silent way, without discussing the position or holding any elections. Despite the protection of group self-maintenance (meetings are held without the mandatory presence of the coordinator), the coordinator inspired and enhanced or weakened the 'pulse' of the group as members leaned on him and sometimes waited for the initiative from him. During the writing of this chapter, the current coordinator started a discussion about leadership, as he felt that it is important for him to leave this position and create a change in the group. Members decided that this role is required as the person who will organize and offer the necessary 'energy', and in terms of ELSiTO coordination should be taken on by all members consecutively by anyone who wishes to try. Each coordinator may take on this role for varying periods of time, a meeting or a short period of time. In this way, members will be involved actively in all aspects of the life of the group.

Epilogue

We continue the ELSiTO group because we have found meaning in it. We are a working group and a companionship at the same time and we have managed to come closer and enjoy what we are doing. We know that everybody is there for each other and will help if needed. The group has changed over time and has had difficult times when a member decided to leave the group for various reasons (personal difficulties, no more meaning of the group, stressfulness, lack of time, immigration).

In the ELSiTO group it is remarkable that the members accept their broader social role, feel equal and do not want to be stigmatized by their status, either as a user or a therapist. They give their knowledge and their experience without expecting anything in return, in their effort to know themselves, the others and the group as a whole and what it can accomplish. A desire of the group members is to spread the uniqueness of ELSiTO, challenging therapists and the broader social network for social inclusion. For those who wish to start a group such as ELSiTO, we invite them to rethink their current practice and their beliefs and to promote social inclusion among professionals, service users, their families and community members as an equal and fair participation in occupations.

Endnotes

1. The programme's partners were:
    *   The Hellenic Association of Occupational Therapists, Greece,
    *   Actenz GGZ in Geest partner VUmc, Amsterdam, The Netherlands and
    *   Hogeschool – Universiteit Brussel, Belgium.
    Collaborative partners were the University of Ruse-Bulgaria, Universitat de Vic-Spain, University of Teeside-UK and the European Network of Occupational Therapy in Higher Education (ENOTHE). Local partners were in Greece: The Municipality of Iraklion Attikis-Centre of Ergotherapy Services and the Panhellenic Union for Psychosocial Rehabilitation and Work Integration (PEPSAEE). In Belgium: the café Polparol-Leuven.
2. Presentations were made to these national and international congresses: Hellenic Congress of Occupational Therapy 2010, World Federation of Occupational Therapists Congress 2010, Council of Occupational Therapists in European Countries Congress 2012, American Association of Occupational Therapists Congress 2013, College of Occupational Therapists Annual Conference 2013, and International Chief Health Professions Officers (ICHPO) – Virtual day of Allied Health & Rehabilitation 2015.
3. A form of direct democracy in ancient Greece was practiced in the ancient city-state of Athens for about 100 years. All adult citizens had to take an active part in government (rule by many) if called on to do so. This form of government is called a direct democracy. The Athenian leader, Pericles, said: 'It is true that we (Athenians) are called a democracy,

for the administration is in the hands of the many and not the few, with equal justice to all alike in their private disputes.'

References

Ammeraal, M., Kantartzis, S. and Vercruysse. L. (Eds) (2011) *Doing Social Inclusion. ELSiTO*. Amsterdam: Uitgeverij Tobi Vroegh

Ammeraal, M., Kantartzis, S., Burger, M., Bogeas, T., van der Molen, C. and Vercruysse, L. (2013) ELSiTO. A collaborative European initiative to foster social inclusion with persons experiencing mental illness. *Occupational Therapy International*. 20, 68–77

ELSiTO (2015) *ELSiTO. Empowering learning for social inclusion through occupation*. [Accessed 15 December 2015 at www.elsito.net]

Kantartzis, S., Ammeraal, M., Breedveld, S., Mattijs, L., Geert, Leonardos, Yiannis, Stefanos and Georgia (2012) 'Doing' social inclusion with ELSiTO: Empowering learning for social inclusion through occupation. *Work*. 41, 447–454

Νικάκη, I. and Μπογέας Θ. (2010) Η εκπαιδευτική σύμπραξη μέσα από το έργο: ELSITO. Εργοθεραπεία. 43, 89-94. [Nikaki, I. and Bogeas, T. (2010) A learning partnership through occupation: ELSITO. *Ergotherapeia*, 43, 89-94]

Chapter 2
Enabling social inclusion through occupation with refugees: A perspective from education

Patricia Eyres, Fiona Fraser, Marnie Smith, Susie Dent,
Miranda Cunningham, Margaret Jelley, Rebecca Twinley,
Lyn Westcott, Anita Slade, Katrina Bannigan

Introduction

What differentiates occupational therapists from other health and wellbeing professionals is their focus on occupation as an agent for personal growth, achievement, and change. It is essential for all occupational therapists to understand what individuals do, both on their own and with others. Therefore, occupation is the cornerstone to both practice and the occupational therapy curriculum (Yerxa, 1998). Occupational therapy education is the gateway to becoming a practising occupational therapist. It is 'through education, students learn to demonstrate their competences in the practice of human occupation through a professionalised discourse' (Pollard & Sakellariou, 2012, p. 27). Wilcock (2007) has encouraged educators to inspire students to shape healthy communities through occupation by 'doing, being, becoming and belonging' where belonging refers to people's interpersonal relationships and level of connectedness to others. Other commentators have referred to 'belonging' as incorporating social interaction, mutually supportive relationships, and having a sense of inclusion (Hammell, 2004; Rebeiro, 2001). Hammell (2014) proposed it is important to explore an individual's need for belonging, within social contexts and occupations. The shift in occupational therapy away from a focus simply on the doing of an occupation to belonging requires an increased understanding of the meaning of the occupation, and its link to health, wellbeing, and social inclusion, both at an individual and community level. This has to be reflected in the occupational therapy curriculum.

The relationship between occupation and health is the threshold concept for occupational therapy, where a 'threshold concept' captures the essential nature of a discipline (Fortune & Kennedy-Jones, 2014). Fortune and Kennedy-Jones (2014, p. 294) urge academics

> 'to reflect on whether the learning environments and conversations created within them enable learners to be transformed in their understanding of the relationship between occupation and health.'

Concomitantly Galheigo (2011) argues that occupational therapists and scientists have an ethical responsibility, and should consider engagement in meaningful occupation as a human right. The profession at the highest level, the World Federation of Occupational Therapists (WFOT), has set global minimum educational standards (2016) alongside position statements of human rights (2019) and competency for practitioners (2008). These standards incorporate other global remits such as the human rights to health agenda of the World Health Organisation (2017). As occupational therapists, who are working to achieve this in our communities, we also need to advocate for this right at a political level, by considering not just the effect but the root cause of occupational injustice. It is therefore incumbent on the education system to prepare the next generation of occupational therapists to engage in social transformation (Duncan & Watson, 2004). Students develop their passion for occupation by experiencing the emancipatory power of occupation through occupational practice (Duncan & Watson, 2004). We need to identify and facilitate educational experiences, including practice experience, to ignite and drive a passion for working with individuals, groups, and communities to promote physical, mental, and social health through occupation. This includes encouraging students to work with different groups of individuals at risk of social exclusion, such as people who are marginalised through social class, literacy and numeracy problems, gender and sexuality issues, mental illness, learning difficulties, physical disabilities or simply their age. Many of these people could be reached through statutory services in the UK unlike some other excluded groups such as people undergoing gender reassignment and young and adult offenders.

Overview of the chapter

In this chapter we explore some of the issues we face, as occupational therapy educators working in the UK, in providing high quality learning experiences that enable students to experience the impact of collective occupation in their local community. We explain how we have capitalised on an opportunity—engagement with a local, charitable organisation: Students and Refugees Together (START)—to realise this ambition. Our work with START is presented as an exemplar of our learning and teaching practice. It demonstrates that an interdisciplinary practice placement, which focuses upon supporting marginalised people within their community, can be a conduit for students to learn about and effect social inclusion through occupation.

Promoting social inclusion in occupational therapy education

The main challenge in promoting social inclusion through occupation, for occupational therapy educators in the UK, is the highly regulated statutory health and social care system. It involves a range of stakeholders, and the majority of learning experiences reflect this. For occupational therapy students, recent changes to the funding available from the National Health Service (NHS), the statutory provider of health services in the UK, has altered the landscape and will potentially alter where students choose to work. To date there has been a focus on working with individuals, within statutory services, with limited opportunity to address social inclusion or health promotion issues. As educators we are mindful of the need to prepare students for the longevity of their practice, changing health priorities and the occupational needs of the population (Wilcock, 2007).

Occupational therapy educators have seized opportunities, like the shortage of practice placements in statutory services, to develop new approaches to learning, such as placements in non-statutory settings (Overton et al, 2009). This ensures that graduates develop the skills they need to adapt to practice in a rapidly changing world as well as have first-hand experience of the difference occupation can make in the lives of communities rather than only for individuals.

The influence of stakeholders in occupational therapy education

The predominantly statutory nature of health and social care in the UK means there are a wide range of stakeholders who have an investment in occupational therapy education. One of these, the UK government, regulates the profession through the Health and Care Professions Council. It, rather than the UK Royal College of Occupational Therapists, approves programmes and holds the register of professionals 'licensed' to practise in the UK. To date the NHS funded education of occupational therapists in the UK has meant that stakeholders' priorities have often focused on skills based interventions to deliver organisational goals (cost efficiencies, financial targets, and integrated care pathways for the individual patient). The value of occupation to communities has not been a priority. Moreover, recent changes to government budgets mean that the NHS will no longer fund occupational therapy education in the UK which will alter the stakeholder landscape in the future, but rooting the education of occupational therapists within an occupational perspective of belonging remains a challenge.

In the midst of this, service users, the most important stakeholders, are at risk of being unheard. The people occupational therapists should be working with, who can be some of the most vulnerable individuals and communities (such as refugees and people with disabilities), are less likely to provide an input into education and service planning. Occupational therapy educators need to provide these groups with the tools to advocate for themselves and find avenues to involve all stakeholders in education.

Facilitating learning to enable social inclusion through occupation

A case study of START is described to illustrate how learning can be facilitated to enable social inclusion through occupation. START works in partnership with individuals and families using activities to reduce social isolation, facilitate learning and to encourage personal and professional development (see Overview of START's work below). The needs of refugees at START include receiving information, practical support, access to existing services and integration into the community (Butler, 2005). START has a unique staffing structure which '... harnesses the enthusiasm, time and humanity of students on professional courses and creates possibility where none seems to exist' (START, 2015). The service operates with three full time members of staff who provide supervision and guidance to students, drawn from occupational therapy, social work, international relations, geography, clinical psychology and law, together with health and social care programmes, who are placed within the setting. The students work collaboratively and participate in placements throughout the year and so form the main body of the workforce. In order to maintain the service through the summer, START often employs students, which provides an additional opportunity for them to gain experience that will enhance their work as occupational therapists when they graduate. Without the student workforce model START would not be financially viable (START, 2015). In the 10 years to 2013, 189 student placements had taken place working with 2500 people (START, 2015) representing a long and successful use of this placement model.

Overview of START's work

Students and Refugees Together (START) is a third sector organisation founded in 2001, when Plymouth became one of the UK government's dispersal areas for refugees. The people that START works with, come from a wide range of nationalities and more than 40 languages have been spoken in the service, however more than 50% of people come from the nations of Eritrea, Iran, Sudan and Kurdistan. START exists to 'to work in partnership with families, individuals and organisations to facilitate the transition of refugees from people in need to self-reliant contributors to their local communities' (START, 2015). The intention is to support refugees in a culturally relevant way 'giving what they need, just when they need it' (START, 2015). Its services include:

- An information access point - available to all refugees.
- Job club – 50+ people attend the weekly session. They need to evidence job searching to access benefits. Advice includes writing a CV, interview culture, and completing application forms. This complements courses run to maximise people's access to employment such as 'First aid in the workplace' and food hygiene certificated programmes.
- One-to-one casework – students work with individual refugees advocating and working with them to secure housing and financial benefits. This service is open to people once they have 'leave to remain' in the UK granted by the Home Office. START works with another local agency to jointly run the Refugee Housing Support Service.
- Community activities – Refugees often find themselves both isolated and occupationally deprived. START runs a number of community activities such as a fortnightly cultural kitchen, where refugees and students cook, eat and talk informally, a women's creative group that meets during school term time, working on projects as varied as banner making, theatre workshops and jewellery making. START also has an allotment; people can have a small plot to grow vegetables and food is grown for the cultural kitchen. A walking group accesses the beautiful Devon countryside regularly. Often people are unfamiliar with the concept that walking is permitted, safe, and can be enjoyable, health promoting as well as a social experience.

START also works on specific projects from time to time such as the resettlement of Afghan interpreters.

Occupational therapy students at the University of Plymouth have the opportunity to work with refugees on a placement with START during their second or third year of study. START is not offered as a first year placement because a firm grasp on theory is needed to fully engage in the learning and to ensure quality of service provision can meet the needs of the refugees. Professional supervision is provided by university staff using an offsite supervision model with students, (i.e. Wood, 2005; COT, 2006). During their placement students work collaboratively with refugees, along with students from different professional backgrounds, to identify immediate needs, assist with housing and other immediate and longer term needs, and advocate for, and with, the refugees (Butler, 2007). The people the students are working with are occupationally deprived in respect to employment. The UK asylum process states that applicants are not allowed to work whilst they are waiting for a decision but must seek work immediately if given 'leave to remain'. The range of occupational opportunities offered by START is varied with individual activities as well as regular group meetings. Group activities, chosen by the whole START community, include tending an allotment (the produce of which is used in the cultural kitchen), needlework projects, culturally diverse cooking, table tennis and walking in the local countryside and coastal paths. These activities, as well as being meaningful to the START community, are accessible, not reliant on proficient language skills, and achieved at minimum cost. By engaging and collaborating with refugees in these activities students can see first-hand the value of health promoting occupation and belonging, and so broaden their understanding of social inclusion by observing social exclusion. They witness the rude and racist behaviour exhibited towards the refugees, the way refugees are treated differently by service providers and the need for the cultural kitchen because of a lack of sense of belonging in the community (Gupta & Sullivan, 2013; Farias & Asaba, 2013). As well as consolidating an understanding of the discrete value of occupational focussed practice to the people they work with, in terms of doing, being, becoming and belonging (Wilcock, 2006), students learn how their skills complement the skills of the other professionals they work alongside.

The students also contribute to the social capital of Plymouth through the social networks, shared values and objectives, and community cohesion (Wilcock, 2006), which START promotes by enabling individuals and groups to engage in mutually trusting and working relationships (Keeley, 2007). As the students form part of START's workforce, they have full responsibility for their work with people they are supporting; they are not shadowing another occupational therapist. They experience first-hand the use of occupation to express and support human flourishing. As this is a reciprocal relationship, with students and refugees problem solving together, refugees find their own skills and experiences are valued. They contribute to the students' knowledge base as well as the solutions required to meet their own needs. Learning is framed as mutually beneficial and refugees are able to contribute more formally to students' education, i.e. by consenting to be the basis for student case study assignments. Together students and refugees collaborate to develop confidence and skills aimed at empowering social inclusion. Skills that enable the refugees to participate in wider society, such as being able to read a bill, book a driving test or arrange a child's school admission, are occupations that refugees and students explore and problem solve together. This can promote a positive environment both for refugees experiencing a new culture in the UK and for students to collaborate and grow solutions together. Recent research carried out by START found that finding work was the highest priority for service users. However, having some social space and opportunities to have 'something to do' were also highlighted as important by service users (START, 2015).

Learning opportunities for students provided by START

A placement with START provides the student with diverse learning opportunities due to the multicultural nature of the environment. UK curriculum guidance (RCOT, 2019) requires that the concept of cultural competency is introduced to occupational therapy students during their studies (Darawsheh, et al, 2015; Haro et al, 2014; Matteliano & Stone, 2014). While on placement at START students deepen their learning about cultural competency and preparedness; 'It is believed that the single most important factor in becoming culturally competent is exposure to culturally diverse situations' (Forwell et al, 2001, p. 92). The START placement enables students to appreciate the complexities first-hand in a real world context. By the time the placement concludes, the students have matured in their ability to appreciate an individual's experience of social exclusion, their distinctive cultural needs, how this influences their occupational needs and the work needed to achieve social inclusion. START provides additional opportunities, from the refugees themselves to explore the complexity of culture, in terms of status and power, colonial history, legal frameworks, racism and discrimination. These are aspects of cultural identity which may otherwise be missing from the curriculum due to time constraints. Students spend time being with refugees, and have an opportunity to move beyond superficial cultural learning by

> '…just interacting, talking and being open to people of different cultures, asking them questions and just trying to understand. Being willing to look for explanations other than you know the obvious ones that you see. Or that you think you see.' (Forwell et al, 2001, p. 100).

Social work students study cultural identity before placement begins and occupational therapy students explore issues of occupational interruption and deprivation across a range of case studies aimed at providing insight into cultural competency. (Logistical constraints mean they do not normally have the opportunity to be taught together). Students also report experiencing 'a culture shock' on this placement because it operates in such a different way to statutory services they have generally been exposed to. On reflection, students felt they became 'more autonomous and independent practitioners'; they embraced possibilities for their future practice, in terms of non-statutory employment and working with socially marginalised members of our communities.

Support is offered to students by on-site staff and off-site supervisors and students are encouraged to use an action learning set model:

'…an approach to individual and organisational development. Working in small groups known as 'sets', students tackle important organisational issues or problems and learn from their attempts to change things.' (Pedler, 2008, p.3).

Students are encouraged to explore their own learning needs, as a staff group, while on placement. At the start of their placement they are able to work alongside students already at START—they often have a period of shadowing to begin their placement—and have peer support from all the students on staff. Close liaison with university educators is maintained to ensure students meet learning goals, use supervision to the greatest effect and develop their professional reasoning. On-site support is combined with weekly individual or group supervision sessions, when students are encouraged to explore their experiences with their supervisor and set on-going objectives.

The START management team has fostered a work culture where staff members are comfortable to say 'I don't know'; this is an essential feature of this placement. The work and the setting are new to students when they arrive—the majority start placement without experience of working alongside refugees. They develop a mature approach to professional learning through being able to say to the refugee 'let's find out together'. This approach may feel different to that of placements experienced within statutory services where collaborative work with students from different professions may be limited and working practices are often ingrained. At START students are encouraged to learn from their experiences to support their future practice and engagement with service users, rather than being anxious about performing perfectly. Confidence and trust amongst staff members, as well as being able to give feedback on the service, engenders the refugees' trust and confidence in the agency. This feature is crucial for collaborative and inclusive working.

Students explore autonomous working as well as benefitting from the open space to gain others' perspectives on cases. The unique staffing structure of START offers an immersive experience of collaborative working and multidisciplinary co-operation and communication. These skills are highlighted repeatedly in reports on high profile communication and organisational breakdowns within health and social care in the UK (e.g., Francis, 2013; Lamming, 2009). Joint working with other agencies is a significant aspect of any placement. Students have voiced surprise at the reaction of others: some agencies were unhelpful and saw refugees as 'hard work' because their cases were seen as complex; they often needed an interpreter, which has implications in terms of barriers to communication and the additional time to organise appointments. This gave students an opportunity to explore, in supervision, issues of discrimination that inhibit social inclusion first-hand. Subsequently they developed skills to advocate for service users, and to educate colleagues. For example, building professional networks with external agencies (such as local statutory, and non-statutory, housing and education services and job centres) and highlighting the needs of refugees. Students often find themselves working alongside START ex-service users, acting as interpreters, which extends the concept of collaborative working. Working so closely with students from different disciplines compels occupational therapy students to identify, articulate and enact their unique role in enabling social inclusion through occupation.

The students' perspective on enabling social inclusion through occupation at START

Following completion of a placement at START, students reflected upon the opportunities for enabling social inclusion through occupation during a group discussion with tutors. The consensus was it was hard to see the focus on occupation at first. This was attributed to it being a non-traditional setting where no on-going, occupationally focused, or based, intervention (by an occupational therapist) was in place. When asked to describe their average week in this setting, students cited advocacy as the main skill and role that was expected of them, and which they primarily performed. Initially the advocacy role was unfamiliar to them; it often involved needing to voice individual refugee's needs (due to language difficulties) to other services and organisations. Students grasped the opportunity and necessity to learn promptly about promoting social inclusion and the occupational needs of the refugees they were working with. Students described how on their placements with START they:

- Made concrete the first three stages of Maslow's (1943) original five-stage model of a hierarchy of needs in terms of their relationship to occupation and health. Specifically, they experienced how refugees' occupational needs were related to: 1) basic biological and physiological needs (such as food, drink, shelter, warmth, and sleep); 2) safety needs (such as protection from the elements, personal security, and freedom from fear); and 3) values related to belonging i.e. the need for family and friends to be with them and to be safe.
- Their work involved supporting refugees with survival occupations, i.e. finding secure housing or financial security, before they could engage in supporting a broader range of occupations. One student said:

  'They didn't want to focus on anything other than finance, housing, and getting a job. Only after that was when they could talk about activities... like the allotment'.

  This allowed students to experience how focussing on survival occupations is necessary to enable people to survive particularly in a new and changing environment (Ede, 2008). Other activities, such as leisure, are not necessarily meaningful until survival has been achieved.
- Engaged with enabling refugees to become integrated into their (new) community. For example, one student supported a female with children to organise childcare; she was then able to arrange attendance on a college course to develop her English language skills.
- Observed how occupational opportunities, such as playing football or having a meal together, are linked to increasing wellbeing and gaining a sense of connectedness. This in turn gave them confidence in the power of occupation to facilitate wellbeing and the development of new identities that have meaning within a new host community and new surroundings.
- Gained insight into the experience of other people's lives and, at the same time, considered their own lives; refugees' journeys to the UK are long and challenging, and students felt it was hard to understand what people had been through.

- Learnt about cultural differences but, especially, about how it shapes people's decisions, choices, and identity. Specifically, students observed how refugees' occupational identities were formed by their choices and the cultural context within which they now lived; their considerations about this echoed Kielhofner's (2008, p. 106) suggestion that occupational identity is

> '... a composite sense of who one is and wishes to become as an occupational being generated from one's history of occupational participation'. One student expressed how the experience impacted directly upon her sense of self, commenting: 'I have a stronger sense of self – it reminded me of who I am. Culture is who you are'.

This case study is one example of how the curriculum at Plymouth University is teaching occupation and social inclusion. Such practice experiences prepare future occupational therapy practitioners by enabling them to develop their professional identity, behaviour, and competence (Mason & Bull, 2006). Indeed, AOTA (2007) propose that professional power is dependent on positive educational outcomes for occupational therapy students. Whilst the students initially felt challenged by the freedom and need to work autonomously at START, they gained confidence which will form the bedrock of their future practice. One student felt they prepared to be 'adaptable as occupational therapists to work with the here and now of a person's lived experience'. Being stretched, with on-site and off-site supervision, provides a challenging learning experience that enables students to acquire skills whilst also contributing to the social capital of their local community. This also goes some way towards the students' understanding that they are not tourists in the lives of the refugees they are working with; that the experience is reciprocal.

The wider curriculum and curriculum design

This case study, about enabling social inclusion through occupation, is one example of how this is achieved, in one occupational therapy programme, in one country, and as such could be atypical. Similar approaches are used in other parts of the world, e.g. South Africa (Lorenzo & Buchanan, 2006), and documented by others e.g. Windley (2011). This suggests these learning opportunities have merit, particularly where student involvement is sustained and has positive impact for service users and their community over a period of time. It was useful to concentrate on a contemporary, non-statutory placement to illustrate the richness of the learning opportunity offered but it is not the whole story. Whilst such non-statutory placements have been recognised as providing students with the opportunity to see the role and value of occupation (Clarke et al, 2014) if this was the only opportunity for students to explore occupation to enable social inclusion, academics would be giving lip service to exploring the potential of occupation.

Innovation in practice education is one aspect of the curriculum that sits alongside, and is complemented by, a wider scheme of occupationally driven occupational therapy study. Involving occupationally focussed practitioners, i.e. occupational therapists who maintain occupation at the heart of their practice, in the teaching of students also has a role to play (Gillen & Greber, 2014) in order to realise the learning potential of such placements.

From a curriculum design perspective, the use of problem based learning is also an effective method of promoting creative thinking and innovative practice (Riley & Matheson, 2010), including facilitation of skills and commitment to occupationally focused working. Making sense and realising the possibilities of placements like those at START in an occupational way are complemented by university study that facilitates discussion embracing the fundamental importance of occupation. Curriculum design, as well as innovative learning opportunities, is used to enable students to develop the intellectual dexterity required for promoting and delivering practice promoting health and wellbeing in an ever changing world (Scaffa & Wooster, 2004; Royeen, 1995). However redesigning curricula to support occupationally driven working may involve culture-change, which can be a slow process with so many stakeholders. This explains, in part, why there is sometimes a gap between what exists and what is needed (Rudman, 2014).

Conclusion

This chapter has outlined the challenges and opportunities for delivering occupational therapy programmes which value and emphasise students' exploration of occupation specifically for needs arising from social rather than medical issues. Academics, working in highly regulated settings, such as the UK, have to meet the needs of a wide range of stakeholders whose mandates can constrain the curriculum. A placement shortage within statutory services was the key driver in the development of non-statutory student placements in the UK. This opportunistic development has allowed students to learn about engaging in sustainable and meaningful work with service users and their communities and has shown how these learning experiences have enriched occupational therapy education in the UK. Education has the potential to provide students' with the experience of enabling social inclusion through occupation for the individuals, groups, and communities they work with.

References

American Occupational Therapy Association. (2007) AOTA's centennial vision and executive summary. *The American Journal of Occupational Therapy*, 61, 613-614

Black, M. (2011) From kites to kitchens: collaborative community-based occupational therapy with refugees survivors of torture. in F. Kronberg, N. Pollard, and D. Sakellariou, (Eds.) *Occupational Therapy without Borders*. Edinburgh: Churchill Livingstone Elsevier (pp 217-225)

Burchett, N. and Matheson, R. (2010) The need for belonging: The impact of restrictions on working on the well-being of an asylum seeker, *Journal of Occupational Science*, 17, 2, 85-91

Butler, A. (2005) A strengths approach to building futures: UK students and refugees together. *Community Development Journal*, 40, 2, 147-157

Butler, A. (2007) Students and refugees together: Towards a model of student practice learning as service provision, *Social Work Education*, 26(3): 233–46.

Clarke, C., Martin, M., Sadlo, G., and de-Visser, R. (2014) The development of an authentic professional identity on role-emergent placements. *British Journal of Occupational Therapy*, 77, 5, 222-229

College of Occupational Therapists. (2006) *Developing the Occupational Therapy Profession: providing new work-based learning opportunities for students. College of Occupational Therapists Guidance 4.* London: College of Occupational Therapists

Duncan, M. and Watson, R. (2004) Transformation through occupation: Towards a prototype. in: R. Watson, and L. Swartz (Eds.) *Transformation through Occupation*. London: Whurr (pp.301-318).

Darawsheh, C., Chard, G., and Eklund, M. (2015) The challenge of cultural competency in the multicultural 21st Century: A conceptual model to guide occupational therapy practice. *The Open Journal of Occupational Therapy*, 3, 2, Article 5 [Accessed 29 October 2015 at http://dx.doi.org/10.15453/2168-6408.1147]

Ede, J. (2008) The art of occupation in: E. McKay, C. Craik, K. Hean Lim, and G, Richards (Eds.) *Advancing Occupational Therapy in Mental Health Practice*. Oxford: Wiley-Blackwell (pp. 118-131)

Farias, L., and Asaba, E (2013) 'The family knot': Negotiating identities and cultural values through the everyday occupations of an immigrant family in Sweden, *Journal of Occupational Science*, 20:1, 36-47

Fortune, T. and Kennedy-Jones, M. (2014) Occupation and its relationship with health and wellbeing: The threshold concept for occupational therapy. *Australian Occupational Therapy Journal*, 61, 5, 293-8

Forwell, S.J., Whiteford, G., and Dyck, I. (2001) Cultural competence in New Zealand and Canada: Occupational therapy students' reflections on class and fieldwork curriculum *Canadian Journal of Occupational Therapy*, 68, 2, 90-103

Francis, R. (2013) *Report of the Mid Staffordshire NHS Foundation Trust Public Inquiry: executive summary*. London: Stationery Office

Galheigo, S.M. (2011) What needs to be done? Occupational therapy responsibilities and challenges regarding human rights. *Australian Occupational Therapy Journal*, 58, 2, 60–66

Gillen, A. and Greber, C. (2014) Occupation-focused practice: Challenges and choices. *British Journal of Occupational Therapy*, 77, 1, 39 – 41

Gupta, J. and Sullivan, C. (2013) The central role of occupation in the doing, being and belonging of immigrant women, *Journal of Occupational Science*, 20, 1, 23-35

Hammell, K.W. (2004) Dimensions of meaning in the occupations of daily life. *Canadian Journal of Occupational Therapy*, 71, 5, 296-305

Hammell, K.W. (2014) Belonging, occupation, and human well-being: An exploration. *Canadian Journal of Occupational Therapy*, 81, 1, 39-50

Haro, A.V., Knight, B.P., Cameron, D.L., Nixon, S.A., Ahluwalia, P.A., and Hicks, E.L. (2014) Becoming an occupational therapist: Perceived influence of international fieldwork placements on clinical practice. *Canadian Journal of Occupational Therapy*, 81,3, 173-182

Keeley, B. (2007) *OECD Insights: Human Capital: How what you know shapes your life*. Paris: Organisation for Economic Co-Operation and Development.

Kielhofner, G. (2008) Dimensions of doing. in G. Kielhofner (Ed.) *Model of Human Occupation: Theory and application*. Baltimore, MD: Lippincott Williams & Wilkins (pp. 101-109)

Laming, H. (2009) *The Protection of Children in England: A progress report*. London: The Stationery Office

Lorenzo, T. and Buchanan, H. (2006) Working in the real world: Unlocking the potential of students. in T. Lorenzo, M. Duncan, H. Buchanan and A. Alsop (Eds.) *Practice and Service Learning in Occupational Therapy: Enhancing potential in context*. Chichester: John Wiley Ltd (pp. 88-102)

Maslow, A.H. (1943) A theory of human motivation. *Psychological Review*, 50, 4, 370-96

Mason, L.R. and Bull, B.J. (2006) Practice placement education in mental health: the educator's experience. *British Journal of Occupational Therapy*, 69,1, 22-30

Matteliano, M.A. and Stone, J.H. (2014) Cultural competence education in university rehabilitation programs. *Journal of Cultural Diversity*, 21, 3, 112-118

Overton, A., Clark, M.J. and Thomas, Y. (2009) A review of non-traditional occupational therapy practice placement education: A focus on role –emerging and project placements. *British Journal of Occupational Therapy*, 72, 7, 294-301

Pedlar, M. (2008) *Action Learning for Managers* (Revised edition). Farnham: Gower

Pollard, N. and Sakellariou, D. (2012) The language of occupation. in N. Pollard and D. Sakellariou (Eds.) *Politics of Occupation-Centred Practice: Reflections on occupational engagement across cultures*. Oxford: Wiley-Blackwell (pp. 25-41)

Rebeiro, K.L. (2001) Enabling occupation: The importance of an affirming environment. *Canadian Journal of Occupational Therapy*, 68, 2, 80–89

Riley, J. and Matheson, R. (2010) Promoting creative thinking and innovative practice through the use of problem-based learning. in T. Clouston, L. Westcott, S.W. Whitcombe, J. Riley, and R. Matheson (Eds.) *Problem-Based Learning in Health and Social Care*. Oxford: Wiley-Blackwell (pp.125-138)

Royal College of Occupational Therapists (2019) *Learning and Development Standards for Pre-Registration Education*. London: Royal College of Occupational Therapists

Royeen, C.B. (1995) A problem-based learning curriculum for occupational therapy education. *The American Journal of Occupational Therapy*, 49, 4, 338-346

Rudman, D.L. (2014) Embracing and enacting an 'occupational imagination': Occupational science as transformative. *Journal of Occupational Science*, 21, 4, 373-388.

Scaffa, M.E. and Wooster, D.M. (2004) Effects of problem-based learning on clinical reasoning in occupational therapy. *American Journal of Occupational Therapy*, 58, 3, 333-336

Smith, H.C. (2015) An exploration of the meaning of occupation to people who seek asylum in the United Kingdom. *British Journal of Occupational Therapy*, 78, 10, 614-621

START (2015) *START Annual Report 2013-14*. START [Accessed 1 May 2015 at http://www.studentsandrefugeestogether.com/Resources/PublishedDocumentsandReports/Annual%20Report%202013-14.pdf]

Wilcock, A.A. (2006) *An Occupational Perspective of Health*. Thorofare, NJ: Slack

Wilcock, A.A. (2007) Occupation and health: Are they one and the same? *Journal of Occupational Science*, 14, 1, 3-8

Windley, D. (2011) Community development. In M. Thew, M. Edwards, S. Baptiste and M. Molineux (Eds.) *Role Emerging Occupational Therapy: Maximising occupation-focused practice*. Oxford: Wiley-Blackwell

Wood, A. (2005) 'Student practice contexts: Changing face, changing place'. *British Journal of Occupational Therapy*, 68, 8, 375-378.

World Federation of Occupational Therapists. (2002) *Minimum Standards for the Education of Occupational Therapists*. WFOT [Accessed 1 April 2015 at http://www.wfot.org/Store/tabid/61/CategoryID/1/Default.aspx]

World Federation of Occupational Therapists (2016) *Minimum Standards for the Education of Occupational Therapists.* WFOT [Accessed 15 Feb 2021 at https://www.wfot.org/resources/new-minimum-standards-for-the-education-of-occupational-therapists-2016-e-copy] World Federation of Occupational Therapists (2008) *Entry level competencies for occupational therapists.* WFOT [Accessed 1 April 2015 http://www.wfot.org/ResourceCentre.aspx]

World Health Organisation. (2008) *Human Rights, Health and Poverty Reduction Strategies.* World Health Organisation [Accessed 1 April 2015 http://whqlibdoc.who.int/hq/2008/WHO_HR_PUB_08.05_eng.pdf?ua=1]

Yerxa, E. (1998) Occupation: The keystone of a curriculum for a self-defined profession. *The American Journal of Occupational Therapy*, 52, 5, 365-372

Chapter 3
The transformative potential of urban gardening

Sandra Schiller with Frank Auracher, Katrin Bode, Hans-Jürgen Buttlar, Viviane Constabel, Ursula Koselleck, and Carla Liebig

Introduction: Initiative for change in Hildesheim Nordstadt

In this chapter we want to share our experiences with a project that is part of an ongoing urban gardening initiative in a low-income city quarter of Hildesheim (a city of ca. 100,000 inhabitants in Lower Saxony, Germany). The project started in spring 2013 as a cooperation between two community workers, Frank Auracher and Katrin Bode, a university teacher, Sandra Schiller, five Bachelor students in occupational therapy, represented by Viviane Constabel and Carla Liebig, and a number of volunteers, among them Hans-Jürgen Buttlar and Ursula Koselleck.

Nordstadt is a typical inner city quarter that used to be a proud working class quarter; to this day it is characterized by working class housing, and it includes the majority of the city's industrial and commercial areas. Its decline began in the wake of mass unemployment in the manufacturing sector from the late 1970s onwards, which was accelerated by the lack of support structures for immigrant workers. In the 1960s, immigrant workers had been recruited mainly from Turkey, but also from Spain and Italy (Kampen, 1993). Currently, this city quarter has the highest percentage of unemployed persons as well as a large number of single parents, mentally ill people and immigrants (Elections and Statistics Office Hildesheim, 2016). The number of immigrants multiplied in the late 1990s due to an increased number of refugees, not least because the city's only centralized refugee shelter is located here. Family affiliations and the process of identity building in a foreign country explain to a large extent why people with diverse national backgrounds have settled in this city quarter. The quarter's community worker Frank Auracher has been focussing on the hidden assets and strengths of the inhabitants and of local institutions, trying to activate and motivate them to become more self-organized and interconnected, working as a facilitator for more inclusion and participation. In his view, community development is based on an emphasis on the opportunities which are associated with a diverse population and on the willingness of individuals to see their experiences of distress as a drive for change, an incentive for wanting to have an impact on the environment.

In February 2013 a Future Conference based on the future search method (Weisbord & Janoff, 2010) was organized for inhabitants and stakeholders as an invitation to commit themselves to bringing about change in a specific area over the course of the next years. The Future Conference was organized by Frank Auracher after a world café and an activating survey in several streets in the quarter had resulted in the locating of various areas that the inhabitants of Nordstadt felt should be addressed in the process of community development. Inhabitants who had already committed themselves to getting active in these areas expressed the wish to find new allies. During the Future Conference, 'encounters in diversity' (*Begegnung in Vielfalt*) was identified by the participants as *the* most essential overall theme for innovation. Ideas were generated for how people with diverse backgrounds and talents could get active together to create more opportunities to promote participation and inclusion. One specific aspect was making better use of the existing accessible open green spaces in the community (tidying up the public park, improving the football pitch etc.) and creating more of them.

In reaction to the outcome of the Future Conference, Frank Auracher and Sandra Schiller started a collaboration to facilitate urban gardening initiatives in Nordstadt with an emphasis on the potential role of collective occupations to promote social health and well-being. In this chapter, we reflect on the experiences gained with the first elective student project, which ran from April to December 2013 with five undergraduate students in occupational therapy.

Urban gardening:
Promoting health and well-being, advocating for social change

Urban Gardening is part of a larger grassroots movement that has been gaining popularity as a way of changing the physical environment and reflecting the values of an ecologically sustainable society (Müller, 2012; De La Salle & Holland, 2010; Taborsky, 2008; Redwood, 2009; Meyer-Renschhausen & Holl, 2000). With its various physical and organizational forms it has multiplied the possibilities offered by traditional gardening in home gardens or allotment groups. Shared characteristics are the cultivation of land in urban areas or their periphery and the close connection to the social, ecological and economic conditions of the city.

Horticultural therapy, i.e. the use of plants and gardening activities 'as a medium through which certain clinically defined goals may be met' (Growth Point 1999, cited in Aldridge and Sempik, 2002, p.1), has been used for some time in occupational therapy in Germany (as in other countries), most prominently in geriatrics, physical rehabilitation and mental health. Here the main interest is on the curative and rehabilitative effect gardening has on individual persons in a therapy or hospital garden (Schneiter-Ulmann, 2012). Outside the clinical setting, social and therapeutic horticulture (STH) as pursued by social workers, psychologists or occupational therapists e.g. in community or neighbourhood gardens 'is an emerging therapeutic movement, using horticulture-related activities to promote health and wellbeing of disabled and vulnerable people' (Diamant & Waterhouse, 2010, p.84). Authors from a wide range of disciplines have explored the connection between gardens, gardening participation and health, i.e. its potential to promote health (through improved nutrition, promotion of physical activity and psychological benefits of the natural environment), personal development and social cohesion (Schiller et al, 2014; York

& Wiseman, 2012; Diamant & Waterhouse, 2010; Sempik et al, 2008; Stein, 2008; Haller & Kramer, 2006). Particular attention has been directed to the 'place-based social processes' typically found in community gardens that support collective efficacy (Teig et al, 2009, p.1115). Research in community gardening projects has shown how this creates a feeling of self-efficacy and self-empowerment (Baier, 2013). Gardens are seen as environments for meeting and learning, for cooperation and networking (Müller, 2012). Sharing experiences, developing social skills and applying conflict resolution strategies lead to a sense of empowerment through belonging to a community that can support agency in other areas of life (Taborsky, 2008). As a consequence, community gardens

> 'that intertwine gardening with social, political and economic practices can create broader and more heterogenous learning about social-ecological conditions, and help develop sense-of-place in degraded neighbourhoods' (Bendt et al, 2013, p.18; see also Kingsley & Townsend, 2006; Armstrong, 2000).

In this context, research in occupational therapy has increasingly focused on gardening as an occupation to promote social inclusion, learning from the example of intercultural gardens (Liebig, 2014; Bishop & Purcell, 2013) or gardens for people with disabilities or mental health issues (Hewitt et al, 2013; Simó, 2011). A valuable theoretical basis is offered by Ann Wilcock's occupation-focused eco-sustainable community development approach as:

> 'a holistic, participatory, diverse, and proactive approach that is self-sustaining, based on ecological, biological, natural, social, political and occupational sciences that marry environment, human occupation, and relationships in the most generic form' (Wilcock, 2006, p.226).

In this context, the concepts of doing, being, becoming and belonging (Wilcock, 2006) have turned out to be a useful basis for analysing the meanings of gardening as an occupation (Bishop & Purcell, 2013; Diamant & Waterhouse, 2010). Looking at the relationship between gardeners and their environment, Diamant and Waterhouse (2010) emphasized the value of Wilcock's understanding of the role of the occupational therapist as the broker between individual and environment who promotes a sense of belonging that contributes to health, well-being and social inclusion. Reflecting the relationship with society, a gardening project in Spain considered gardening with socially excluded persons as a medium for social transformation, linking it to the question of promoting occupational justice and the creation of inclusive communities (Simó, 2011).

In addition to addressing issues of social inclusion and occupational alienation, urban gardening tries to change the urban landscape; it is a means of democratization as people engage in appropriating public space to actively shape the environment (Müller, 2012). New forms of working and living are explored, participation and shared decision-making, appropriation and shaping of space are central points as well as empowerment and new concepts of governance (Stierand, 2012). Some gardening projects directly address certain marginalized groups in society, as the example of the successful intercultural garden movement in Germany shows (Baier, 2013; Müller, 2002), while other projects are started in disadvantaged communities to appeal to the local inhabitants in general (e.g. Middling et al, 2011; Ohmer et al, 2009; Wakefield et al, 2007). The philosophy underlying urban gardening can be characterized as a deliberate counterdraft to the neoliberal ideal of agency, i.e. the individual person's capacity for autonomous decision-making – which expediently ignores the situation of people whose socio-economic position or state of health limits their potential for self-reliance and self-sufficiency (Vahsen, 2014). Regarding its political dimension, urban gardening has close connections to the Right to the City movement, as a collective approach to bring about a shift in values towards more social justice in the use of public space (Mitchell, 2014). In this context, community gardens can make a positive contribution to community development, and research from various disciplines has been concerned with social interactions, social networks and social processes in community gardens as well as the collective management of public green spaces by civil society groups (Ghose & Pettygrove, 2014; Bendt et al, 2013; Bartolomei et al, 2003). Accordingly, we are interested in the potential of urban gardening as a social initiative bringing people from various backgrounds together to experience a sense of collective agency. This means focusing on the potential of collective occupations as a medium for creating diverse communities and contributing to social transformation, based on an understanding that communities in low-income neighbourhoods face particular difficulties but also have their very distinct potential to offer. As low-income city quarters are typically characterized by scarce and unappealing space for encounters in public, urban gardening can be understood as a health promotion strategy, in the sense of the WHO (1986) Ottawa Charter's appeal to 'create supportive environments.'

Starting urban gardening in Hildesheim Nordstadt: Rationale for a joint university-community project

Understanding how occupations can foster social inclusion to enhance quality of life is part of a new direction in occupational therapy education to teach students to be able to work with groups, gain an understanding of the relevance of health promotion initiatives, consider social and political contexts of occupations and use a participatory approach focussing on enablement/empowerment (Schiller, 2012; Lauckner et al, 2011; Whiteford & Townsend, 2011; Leclair, 2010; Pollard et al, 2009). Accordingly, taking part in an urban gardening initiative in Hildesheim Nordstadt was to provide the students with an opportunity to make a connection between occupational therapy theory and practice by gaining experience in a role-emerging practice setting outside the traditional health care sector.

The first practical step for the students was to get to know the social geography of the city quarter by locating the public and semi-public spaces potentially suitable for gardening activities. As a next step, they decided to provide a practical example how local space could be used for gardening. Frank Auracher drew the group's attention to the so-called *Nachbarschaftsladen* (Neighbourhood Shop). This is a meeting place in a former bakery run by *zeitreich*, a neighbourhood assistance initiative offering mutual assistance on a voluntary basis and organizing all sorts of group activities (see e. g. Reutlinger et al, 2015; Hill, 2009; on the role of such initiatives in contemporary society). The *Nachbarschaftsladen* is an easily accessible, open and low-threshold contact point to facilitate cooperation and networking and to help integrate marginalized individuals and groups into society by supporting them in their daily life and in developing personal skills. The team of *Nachbarschaftsladen*, consisting of professionals and volunteers, most of whom are simultaneously service users of *zeitreich*, wanted to make the space in front of the building more inviting and to offer a small-scale gardening opportunity to some volunteers who expressed an interest in this occupation but were unable to look after a garden of their own. We saw this as an excellent opportunity. Since *Nachbarschaftsladen* is well-known in the quarter and located in a busy street, we were of the opinion that building a raised garden bed in front of it was a useful, high-profile kick-off project for a larger urban gardening initiative.

Photo 1: The location: The Nachbarschaftsladen

Students and volunteers get active together: Building the raised garden bed

In their first meeting with the team from *Nachbarschaftsladen*, the students introduced the idea of jointly building a raised garden bed in front of the building, which was met with spontaneous enthusiasm. Katrin Bode, the church deacon and community worker responsible for the neighbourhood assistance initiative *zeitreich*, and the rest of the team were willing to take the risk and asked the owner of the premises for permission to go ahead with the project, even though they were worried about the costs associated not just with building and maintaining such a raised garden bed but also about the costs for disposing of it if the project did not go well or if it did not find the approval of the neighbourhood but was vandalized.

The students introduced the idea of a raised garden bed to *Nachbarschaftsladen*'s forum of professionals and volunteers. They had to do research to gain knowledge on raised garden beds and be able to make suggestions on how best to build such a construction in this particular location (e.g. regarding the construction draft, recommended building materials, plants, necessary tools for the construction process etc.) that were then discussed in a joint decision-making process in the whole project group. Students and volunteers from *Nachbarschaftsladen* then contacted potential sponsors (e.g. local building supplies stores and nurseries). Additionally, *zeitreich*, Frank Auracher's community development initiative and the city quarter council provided financial assistance for the materials that had to be purchased. A date was set in early July 2013 where the actual construction process was to take place and *zeitreich*'s secretary went through their list of volunteers to invite everybody with craft skills or manual dexterity. On the fixed day the team of students and volunteers put the wooden construction for the raised garden bed together from scratch, coated it with pool liner, stabilized the frame with cross-bracings and filled it with drainage material. The soil was delivered a couple of days later and finally flowers, vegetables and herbs, many of which had been donated by various people, were planted. Overall, the students and volunteers from *Nachbarschaftsladen* worked together on the project over a period of time stretching from the first meeting in May 2013 to a harvest festival celebrating the end of the project in late September 2013.

Photo 2: Constructing the raised bed

When students and volunteers reflected independently from each other on the quality of their cooperation during the construction phase, they both emphasized the following types of collective occupations as having been important for bringing them together as a team: a) planning, exchanging ideas and reaching agreements, b) craft activities and manual tasks, c) the time spent together having meals, drinking coffee, smoking, etc. In their opinion, what worked in favour of the project was the fact that there was a positive atmosphere right from the start, that everybody was highly motivated and that they did not only focus on working but also on having a good time together – e.g. inviting people from the neighbourhood to celebrate the harvest festival was considered important. In the words of Hans-Jürgen Buttlar, 'the students had fun and it was fun working together with them.' The volunteers from *Nachbarschaftsladen* realized that this was an enjoyable new kind of intergenerational teamwork, as they had never been in contact with students before in this setting.

The students initially expected more self-initiative on the part of the volunteers and instead found themselves pushed into the role of experts. The students were expected to take the lead as *Nachbarschaftsladen* depends on external input and support to start more ambitious new projects. The volunteers are often overwhelmed by such a project. They had no knowledge regarding the construction of a raised bed and as most of them do not have internet access, they would have found it difficult to locate the necessary information. On the other hand, the discussions with the students in the forum made them feel included in the process, created enthusiasm and helped them to think about their gardening interests. Even though the students realized that they initially had to fulfil their expert roles to some extent to get the project rolling, they tried to follow a community development approach based on partnership and equality (see the critical perspective in e.g. Leclair, 2010 and Lauckner et al, 2011; practical guidelines are provided by Galvaan & Peters, 2014 and Zinkstok & Schiller, 2014). The longer the project continued, the more did a different distribution of roles indeed come about. When the volunteers realized during the construction phase that their contribution was met with genuine appreciation and respect, the nature of the collaboration changed. As there were no experts on woodworking in the team, the construction process showed that some of the preparation had been lacking in detail and that the necessary expertise was not always at hand. However, we learned that it was exactly these glitches during the process that made it possible for everybody to experience their competency as a team, because all the various problems were ultimately dealt with successfully. The project assumed a strongly interactive nature and gained support from many different helpers, experts and sponsors, facilitated by the fact that it took place in an open setting and thus attracted a lot of public attention. The participants were delighted how many people in the neighbourhood with diverse skills and connections were willing to help. For example, the soil was spontaneously donated by a landscaping company and a worker with a mechanical digger who happened to be in the neighbourhood when the soil was delivered scooped it into the raised bed – sparing the group hours of manual shoveling. Katrin Bode was surprised about the many personal resources available in the neighbourhood that only got activated because a need for them became visible.

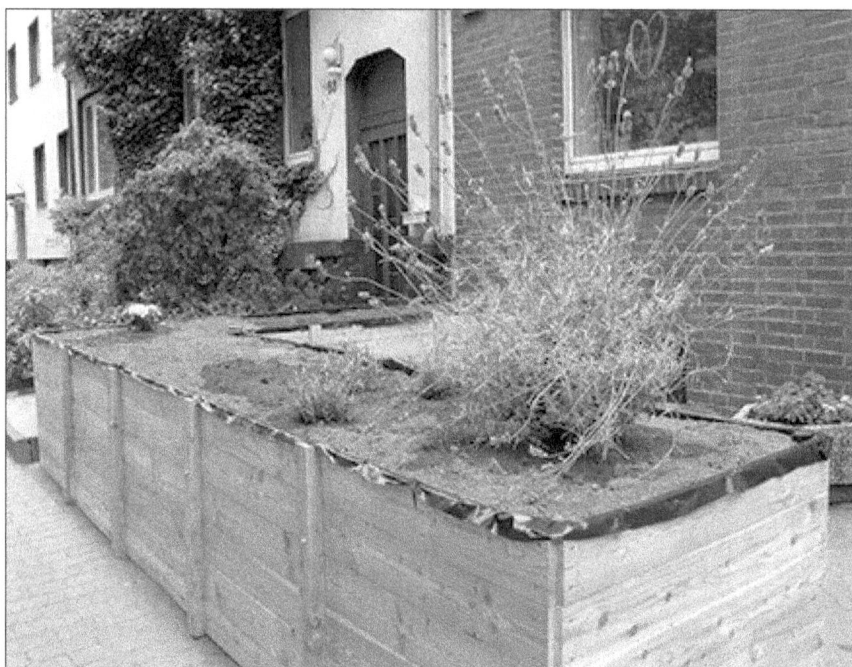

Photo 3: The complete flower bed

Collective occupations, use of space and opportunities for participation created by the raised garden bed

Recently, the 'occupational nature of social groups' (Christiansen & Townsend, 2010, p.176) has received more systematic attention in occupational science literature (e.g. Ramugondo & Kronenberg, 2015; Kantartzis, 2013; Peralta-Catipon, 2012; Fogelberg & Frauwirth, 2010). In order to understand urban gardening appropriately from an occupation-based perspective, Schiller and Dennhardt (2014) suggested expanding the approach by Simó (2011), which considers the dimensions of social interaction and citizenship, to include a systematic exploration of gardening as a collective occupation. While local communities have been undergoing significant structural changes, they still exist and shape the social environment – and in communities in low-income city districts even small gestures of participation are an important achievement (Vahsen, 2014). An analysis of collective occupations should therefore appreciate the role of everyday occupations for maintaining community life, as doing things for others and with others (Kantartzis, 2013).

In addition to the reflection on the immediate construction process as a joint cooperation between students and volunteers, it has been interesting to see the effect the raised garden bed has had on the neighbourhood over the course of the last two years and which occasions for collective occupation it has created that contribute to fostering a sense of community. Here we want to differentiate between: regular occupations; resource orientation; and effects on the environment, i.e. social interaction in an open, public setting.

The regular tasks and occupations associated with gardening (e.g. planting, watering the plants, harvesting) and maintaining the wooden construction (e.g. painting the boards) are primarily the shared responsibility of Hans-Jürgen Buttlar and Ursula Koselleck, who live in the immediate neighbourhood. Neither of them has a garden or balcony but they both used to garden when they were younger and have some basic gardening knowledge. Looking after the raised bed means that they need to walk there to check on it every day, which not only provides them with regular physical activity but also contributes to their daily structure and is an occasion for social contacts. They describe this as a nice occupation, a nice responsibility that is fun. In addition to these benefits, they are proud of the positive feedback they receive from passers-by. All the team from *Nachbarschaftsladen* have had the experience that whenever somebody is outside working on the raised garden bed, this attracts spontaneous offers of support from passers-by, who are on their way to go shopping or visit friends in the neighbourhood, or people living in the neighbourhood. They see these activities going on and are prepared to dedicate some time – as a result, different people collaborate in various gardening activities. According to Katrin Bode, this creates cooperation and teamwork among inhabitants of the quarter – among people who already know each other, but also among strangers. Often even people riding a bike stop to take a closer look. In fact, the raised bed has created its own 'community of gardeners' as people start a conversation and show an interest in the flowers and vegetables, give gardening tips or talk about their memories associated with gardening. Sometimes people bring donations or stake flowers that have been blown over in the wind.

Resource orientation is a common effect of intercultural community gardening that we also consider a crucial long-term effect of our project since people contribute their skills, experiences and knowledge to caring for the raised garden bed in different ways. The spontaneous exchange of gardening tips around the raised bed has shown that there is an interest in gardening knowledge and skills in the neighbourhood. *Nachbarschaftsladen* has started to host meetings for healthy gardening tips or consultations with a gardening expert and is planning cooperation with the recently founded community garden in the neighbourhood. The shared consumption of vegetables grown in the raised garden during neighbourhood parties organized by *Nachbarschaftsladen* (e.g. harvest festival or summer barbecue) makes people aware of the resources created in their community. Furthermore, the consumption of self-grown food contributes to a spreading awareness of 'green issues'. Resource orientation also means using urban gardening to increase people's identification with the city quarter and with changes they have brought about. Hans-Jürgen Buttlar and Ursula Koselleck keep experimenting with which flowers and vegetables are suitable for the raised bed and have developed a more relaxed attitude towards gardening failures in their conversations with other garden lovers. They also use the opportunity to discuss their gardening experiences at parties in the new community garden in the quarter. However, a more conscious effort to see the raised garden bed as part of a network of urban gardening projects in Nordstadt giving presentations on sustainabilty, selling plants or giving advice to consumers, depends on the dedication of the professionals working for *Nachbarschaftsladen*.

A crucial aspect of Frank Auracher's community development initiative has been the creation of documentation and narratives to sustain connectedness through tradition, e.g. by having the construction of the raised garden bed documented by a photographer and by organizing an oral history café dedicated to the personal meanings of gardening. He thinks that the collaboration of students adds an important external resource to the quarter as they dedicate their time, show their appreciation of the inhabitants and introduce innovations. In addition to various projects with the university's social work programme, Frank Auracher has cooperated with Sandra Schiller in a number of health education projects (on the benefits of such partnerships see e.g. Sabo, 2015). University projects can increase the quarter's appeal to students as a place of residence or as a place for their social and cultural commitment, which makes Nordstadt livelier and more diverse.

Photo 4: Opening up a space

Has the construction of the raised garden bed created a feeling of community and a sense of agency regarding the environment? The appropriation of public space has mainly had the following three positive effects: It has drawn more attention to *Nachbarschaftsladen*, because a raised garden bed with vegetables next to a busy street is an unusual sight that gives people something to talk about. In the words of Katrin Bode, 'the raised bed is a great eye-catcher.' During the warmer period it is used as a 'green antechamber', i.e. meetings and group activities often take place in the new seating area outside which the raised bed now shelters from the noise and exhaust fumes of the traffic in the street. This space has a friendly and homey atmosphere, it is a nice place to sit down and have a coffee, provides a sheltered corner for children to play in, and acts as a communication forum for the neighbourhood. The team of service users and professionals feel that it has become easier to start a conversation with people passing by as there is no threshold to cross. In contemporary post-industrial society community development initiatives need to take into consideration that the most significant skill of living and doing together in community is learning to deal with pluralism and diversity and negotiating difference, conflict and dissent (Mouffe, 2000). The raised bed has been a step towards opening up the space outside and increasing the appeal *Nachbarschaftsladen* has on the area – Katrin Bode calls it 'as colourful, diverse and meaningful as the neighbourhood it is located in.'

The immediate neighbours agree that the raised garden bed has improved their surroundings and added to a positive atmosphere in the neighbourhood. Initially they were sceptical that the raised bed would prove hard to maintain and invite acts of vandalism. Now it is seen as a symbol that something is done to improve the surroundings. This reflects an important aim of community development: giving people the experience that they can have a positive impact on their environment (Gilchrist & Taylor, 2011). Through this process they can learn that achievements can be made on a practical level, that they have the power and the skills to do so in teamwork and that they can change their living conditions. Ursula Koselleck mentions a service user who wanted to join in when the boards were given a new coat of paint, so they spontaneously divided up the task, which she sees as 'yet another example of teamwork.' This is motivating and leads to long-term activation, but it is also contagious as it encourages others. The positive effect that the well-maintained raised garden bed has both on the environment and the volunteers is expressed in the following statement by Hans-Jürgen Buttlar:

'Everybody who walks past says: 'This is so beautiful, you've done another great job.' Without wanting to praise myself, when you're there and people tell you such nice things, this gives you rather a boost.'

Generally, any type of occupation can serve as a means of mutual empowerment: If people share an interest in it, this can bring them together and forge a link between them. Urban gardening, however, is particularly useful in this regard because it can have a positive effect on the health and well-being of many people in a city quarter and because it is particularly meaningful to many people of different backgrounds. Hans-Jürgen Buttlar and Ursula Koselleck already have a wealth of anecdotes to share about conversations and interactions with other service users, neighbours and complete strangers around the raised garden bed.

Nevertheless, setbacks caused by vandalism or theft are a particular challenge associated with gardening as an occupation in public space and it needs to be taken into consideration that not every location is equally suited for such projects. This means that we walk a thin line between the pessimistic expectations of many people in a low-income city quarter that such a project is doomed to fail and the need to choose the context of a gardening project in such a way that success can be organized even in the face of intermittent resistance and setbacks. Before the start of the construction phase, Frank Auracher, Katrin Bode and Sandra Schiller emphasized in conversations with the volunteers and with the students that this was a pilot project to test how the inhabitants of *Nordstadt* would react to such an urban gardening initiative and that failure due to vandalism was a possibility. So in addition to the anticipation how the construction process itself would go, there was a lot of curiosity about the long-term development of the project. As community workers, Frank Auracher and Katrin Bode were aware that emotional support needed to be provided to the volunteers, who would find it hard to deal with destroyed or stolen plants. Katrin Bode is convinced that the location of the raised garden bed was well-chosen as *Nachbarschaftsladen* and the raised bed are now accepted as a unity. Ursula Koselleck and Hans-Jürgen Buttlar are happy to report that there have actually been fewer acts of vandalism since the raised bed was finished compared to the time when there were only some flower tubs outside *Nachbarschaftsladen*.

Ever since the raised garden bed was finished in autumn 2013, a growing number of individual persons and community initiatives in the city quarter have started to create small flowerbeds in tree grates on the pavement and a community garden was established. These local projects have been initiated by people with different social backgrounds, predominantly students or artists who want to beautify their city quarter. Hans-Jürgen Buttlar, Ursula Koselleck and the other volunteers from *Nachbarschaftsladen* see this as proof that they had the courage to go first and have provided an example for others so that two years later the positive effect on the city quarter is clearly seen. In a world café organized in November 2015 to collect ideas about improving health in Nordstadt, various participating professionals and inhabitants of the city district mentioned the improvement of the available public space and more green space as an important aspect of health promotion.

Learning experiences:
The role of occupational therapists in creating inclusive community

The students felt that the project provided them with an opportunity to expand their horizons and to acquire some important skills and knowledge regarding occupational therapy practice to promote social health. Viviane Constabel emphasizes that this was the students' first contact with using a community development approach in occupational therapy. In this context, she found that learning about processes of empowerment and about public relations and social entrepreneurship was particularly valuable as many occupational therapists have no expertise in these areas. Likewise, the volunteers expanded their horizons: They educated themselves about gardening and now enjoy passing on their knowledge to others. They have assumed a widely acknowledged task and feel respected.

On a practical level, the students gained experience in how to initiate and facilitate community activities and how to build networks with interested volunteers, sponsors and stakeholders to support a sustainable local start-up project and raise awareness of the overall issue of urban gardening. To encourage collective action many people have to be brought together. The students realized that it is important to formulate a common outcome together with the people you work with. Furthermore it is necessary to clarify and take into consideration the needs and expectations of everyone involved. The students learned that facilitating a collaborative relationship characterized by shared-decision making and aiming at empowerment and participation is a new challenge to occupational therapists working in a community setting. According to Viviane Constabel, their lack of experience at first made it hard for the students to find their role. Reflection at university helped them deal with this: they understood why they initially had to take the lead but that they also had to gradually hand over responsibility to the volunteers and support them in making decisions and initiating activities. In fact, students can only gain an understanding of the potential of collective occupations in the course of such a project, if they have the skills to participate in teamwork with the volunteers. Frank Auracher thinks that the students were ultimately successful in using a community development approach as the experience of working together in practical activities over a longer period of time and the shared feeling of success created the trust that was crucial for a positive long-term effect. In Katrin Bode's view the students were able to motivate the volunteers well by showing them their appreciation and respect. In their reflection both the professionals and the volunteers acknowledged that the students were committed to the project over a long period of time and even on a voluntary basis after the official project phase at university had effectively ended.

On a theoretical level, the students also gained first-hand experience of a community development approach as cooperation between social workers and occupational therapists in this field. They concluded that (urban) gardening turned out to be a meaningful area for occupational therapists aiming to support participation and social inclusion. They developed an understanding of the concept of social health as a result of participation approaches in community development and health promotion. Knowing about and using the commonalities and shared concerns of social work and occupational therapy is key for successful interdisciplinary teamwork. Since they share the aim of promoting inclusive communities and of activating people to self-organized occupations and participation, they are ideally suited for cooperations. Occupational therapists provide an important addition to traditional community work by identifying individual strengths, which is an essential contribution to promoting self-confidence and identification with the individual social environment.

We are convinced that occupational therapists' focus on occupation has added value when dealing with questions of social inclusion, quality of life and well-being in a city quarter. Occupational therapists take into consideration a broad range of contextual factors and try to initiate opportunities for occupation with long-term use and increased independence and self-determination of their service-users in mind. As community workers, both Frank Auracher and Katrin Bode had previously not been aware of the fact that occupational therapists also work with a community development approach to support occupation-based social inclusion. They appreciate occupational therapists' expertise regarding the health benefits of occupations such as gardening, and their access to support systems that can help to include people with physical disabilities or mental health issues in community projects. Similarly, Viviane Constable and Carla Licbig feel that occupational therapists have a wide network of people they work with and that they know the occupational opportunities and needs of people in the city quarter. They can support social inclusion by networking to bring people together based on their interests and potential, e.g. people wishing to get involved in community gardening activities. Their ability to respond to individual occupational challenges, in particular social and communicative difficulties, can contribute to getting people engaged in collective occupations who would not find access to a community or be unable to maintain a long term relationship with their community without the support of an occupational therapist. In this way occupational therapy supports the collective occupations of individuals. This is particularly an issue in city districts where low socio-economic status contributes to processes of social exclusion (Häußermann, 2006). Before the start of the project, the team of professionals and volunteers from *Nachbarschaftsladen* were unaware of the possible benefits of occupational therapy. In hindsight, they feel that gardening has turned out to be a great occupation for the volunteers: It requires not only a lot of regular physical activity, but also cognitive skills since gardening activities need to be planned and organized over the course of the year and planting designs need to be developed. Volunteers Hans-Jürgen Buttlar and Ursula Koselleck confirm that in the course of the project, they have learned to see the role of occupational therapists as professionals who get people activated, get them into physical activity and support them in their essential occupations. Currently, urban gardening projects in Germany often apply for funding from a large range of sponsors and scholarship providers on the local, state and federal level and some intercultural gardens have managed to employ a social worker. This could be a first stepping stone for occupational therapists with a creative project plan and skills in social entrepreneurship (Frei, 2013).

Ultimately, this leads to a critical look at the question of long-term support for urban gardening projects in low-income city quarters. As our example shows, urban gardening does indeed seem to have transformative potential in bringing together people of diverse backgrounds in occasional encounters or regular cooperations. Obviously, enabling everybody to participate in the various opportunities for individual or collective occupation created by the public use of urban gardening spaces, will benefit from the continued 'organization of community' by community workers and occupational therapists.

References

Aldridge, J. and Sempik, J. (2002) *Social and Therapeutic Horticulture: Evidence beyond the messages from research.* Loughborough UniversityCentre for Child and Family Research Evidence Issue 6. [Accessed 30 July 2015 at http://www.greenfingersproject.com/wp-content/uploads/2012/11/Social-and-Therapeutic-Horticulture-Evidences-and-Messages-from-Research.pdf]

Armstrong, D. (2000) A survey of community gardens in upstate New York: Implications for health promotion and community development. *Health & Place*, 6,4, 319–327

Baier, A. (2013) '*Wie soll man gesund sein, wenn man keine Arbeit hat?': Gesundheit und soziale Ungleichheit – Erfahrungen einer Frauengruppe mit einem Gesundheitsprojekt.* Bielefeld: transcript

Bartolomei, L., Corkery, L., Judd, B. and Thompson, S. (2003) *A Bountiful Harvest. Community gardens and neighbourhood renewal in Waterloo.* Univ. of New South Wales [Accessed 30 July 2015 at http://www.be.unsw.edu.au/sites/default/files/upload/pdf/cf/hbep/publications/attachments/A_Bountiful_Harvest.pdf]

Bendt, P., Barthel, S. and Colding, J (2013) Civic greening and environmental learning in public-access community gardens in Berlin. *Landscape and Urban Planning*, 109, 1, 18–30

Bishop, R. and Purcell, E. (2013) The value of an allotment group for refugees. *British Journal of Occupational Therapy*, 76, 6, 264-269

Christiansen, C. H. and Townsend E. A. (2010) The occupational nature of social groups, in C.H. Christiansen and E.A. Townsend (Eds.) *Introduction to Occupation: The art and science of living*. 2nd ed. Upper Saddle River, NJ: Pearson (pp. 175-210)

De La Salle, J. M. and Holland, M. E. (Eds.) (2010) *Agricultural Urbanism: Handbook for building sustainable food systems in 21st century cities*. Winnipeg: Green Frigate Books

Diamant, E. and Waterhouse, A. (2010) Gardening and belonging: Reflections on how social and therapeutic horticulture may facilitate health, wellbeing and inclusion. *British Journal of Occupational Therapy*, 73, 2, 84-88

Elections and Statistics Office Hildesheim (2016). Unpublished data in 'Steckbrief Nordstadt' [received via e-mail in January 2016]

Frei, S. (2013) *Gemeinschaftsgärten als Möglichkeit zur Gesundheitsförderung durch soziale Inklusion: Welchen Beitrag kann die Ergotherapie dazu leisten?* Unpubl. B.Sc. Thesis HAWK Hildesheim/Holzminden/Göttingen

Galvaan, R. and Peters, L. (2014) *Occupation Based Community Development Framework*. [Accessed 30 July 2015 at https://vula.uct.ac.za/access/content/group/9c29ba04-b1ee-49b9-8c85-9a468b556ce2/OBCDF/pages/contact.html]

Ghose, R. and Pettygrove, M. (2014) Actors and networks in urban community garden development. *Geoforum*, 53, 93-103

Gilchrist, A. and Taylor, M. (2011) *The Short Guide to Community Development*. Bristol: The Policy Press

Haller, R. and Kramer, C. (2006) *Horticultural Therapy Methods: Making connections in health care, human service and community programs*. New York: CRC Press

Häußermann, H. (2006) Die Krise der ,'sozialen Stadt': Warum der sozialrämliche Wandel der Städte eine eigenständige Ursache für Ausgrenzung ist. in H. Bude and A. Willisch (Eds.) *Das Problem der Exklusion*. Hamburg: Hamburger Edition (pp. 294-313)

Hewitt, P., Watts, C., Hussey, J., Power, K. and Williams, T. (2013) Does a structured gardening programme improve well-being in young-onset dementia? A preliminary study. *British Journal of Occupational Therapy*, 76, 8, 355-361

Hill, B. (2009) Selbsthilfe, bürgerschaftliches Engagement und sozialräumliche 'Soziale Arbeit', in Deutsche Arbeitsgemeinschaft Selbsthilfegruppen (DAG SHG) e.V. (Ed.) *Selbsthilfegruppenjahrbuch 2009*, 142-155. [Online version accessed 30 July 2015 at http://www.dag-shg.de/data/Fachpublikationen/2009/DAGSHG-Jahrbuch-09-Hill.pdf]

Kampen, S. (1993) Die Entwicklung der Hildesheimer Nordstadt: Ein kurzer Abriss der Siedlungsgeschichte, in Hildesheimer Volkshochschule (Ed.) Die Welt hinter der Bahn: Auf Spurensuche in der Hildesheimer Nordstadt. Hildesheim: Gerstenberg (pp. 18-43)

Kantartzis, S. (2013) *Conceptualising Occupation: An ethnographic study of daily life in a Greek town*. Unpubl. PhD Thesis Leeds Metropolitan University

Kingsley, J. Y. and Townsend, M. (2006) 'Dig in' to social capital: Community gardens as mechanism for growing urban social connectedness. *Urban Policy and Research*, 24, 4, 525–537

Lauckner, H. M., Krupa, T. and Paterson, M. (2011) Conceptualizing community development: Occupational therapy practice at the intersection of health services and community. *Canadian Journal of Occupational Therapy*, 78, 4, 260-268

Leclair, L. L. (2010) Re-examining concepts of occupation and occupation-based models:

Occupational therapy and community development. *Canadian Journal of Occupational Therapy*, 77, 1, 15-21

Liebig, C. (2014) *Gärtnern mit Flüchtlingen: Möglichkeiten der Nutzung von Gemeinschaftsgärten in der gemeinwesenorientierten Ergotherapie.* Unpubl. B.Sc. Thesis HAWK Hildesheim/Holzminden/Göttingen

Meyer-Renschhausen, E. and A. Holl (Eds.) (2000) *Die Wiederkehr der Gärten: Kleinlandwirtschaft im Zeitalter der Globalisierung.* Innsbruck: Studien Verl.

Middling, S., Bailey, J., Maslin-Prothero, S, and Sharf, T. (2011) Gardening and the social engagement of older people. *Working with Older People*, 15, 3, 112-122

Mitchell, D. (2014) *The Right to the City: Social Justice and the Fight for Public Space.* New York, London: The Guilford Press

Mouffe, C. (2000) *The Democratic Paradox.* London: Verso

Müller, C. (2002) *Wurzeln schlagen in der Fremde: Internationale Gärten und ihre Bedeutung für Integrationsprozesse.* Munich: oekom

Müller, C (2012) Urban Gardening: Grüne Signaturen neuer urbaner Zivilisation, in C. Müller (Ed.) *Urban Gardening. Über die Rückkehr der Gärten in die Stadt.* 4th ed. Munich: oekom (pp. 22-53)

Ohmer, M.L., Meadowcroft, P., Freed, F. And Lewiset, E. (2009) Community gardening and community development: Individual, social and community benefits of a community conservation program. *Journal of Community*, 17, 4, 377-99

Peralta-Catipon, T. (2012) Collective occupations among Filipina migrant workers: Bridging disrupted identities. *OTJR: Occupation, Participation and Health*, 32, 2, 14-21

Pollard, N., Sakellariou, D. and Kronenberg, F. (2009) *A Political Practice of Occupational Therapy.* Edinburgh: Elsevier Churchill Livingstone

Ramugondo, E. L. and Kronenberg, F. (2015) Explaining collective occupations from a human relations perspective: Bridging the individual-collective dichotomy. *Journal of Occupational Science*, 22, 1, 3-16

Redwood, M. (2009) *Agriculture in Urban Planning: Generating livelihoods and food security.* London: Earthscan

Reutlinger, C., Stiehler, S. and Lingg, E. (Eds.) (2015) *Soziale Nachbarschaften: Geschichte, Grundlagen, Perspektiven.* Wiesbaden: Springer

Sabo, S., de Zapien, J., Teufel-Shone, N., Rosales, C., Bergsma, L. and Taren, D. (2015) Service learning: A vehicle for building health equity and eliminating health disparities. *American Journal of Public Health*, 105, s1, S38-S43

Schiller, S. (2012) Gemeinwesenorientierung in der Ergotherapie. *Ergotherapie & Rehabilitation*, 51, 3, 24-26

Schiller, S., Blenk, L., Frei, S., Isenbeck, K. and Thies, R. (2014) *'Active Gardening': Intergenerational exploration of healthy gardening strategies for elderly allotment tenants.* Poster at the 16th International Congress of the World Federation of Occupational Therapists: Yokohama, Japan, 18.6.2014

Schiller, S. and Dennhardt, S. (2014) *Collective Occupations as a Way of Fostering a Sense of Citizenship: Looking for meaningful connections between theory and practice in community development – A German perspective.* Presentation at the 2014 Joint International Occupational Science Conference in Minneapolis, Minnesota, USA

Schneiter-Ulmann, R. (2012) Gartentherapie – Begriffe, Entwicklung, Anwendung, in R. Schneiter-Ulmann (Ed.) Lehrbuch Gartentherapie. Bern: Hans Huber (pp. 23-38)

Sempik, J., Aldridge, J. and Becker, S. (2008) *Growing Together: A practice guide to promoting social inclusion through gardening and horticulture*. Bristol: The Policy Press

Simó, S. (2011) Universities and the global change: Inclusive communities, gardening, and citizenship, in F. Kronenberg, N. Pollard and D. Sakellariou (Eds.) *Occupational Therapies without Borders. Vol. 2: Towards an ecology of occupation-based practices*. Edinburgh: Churchill Livingstone Elsevier (pp. 357-365)

Stein, M. (2008) Community gardens for health promotion and disease prevention. *International Journal for Human Caring*, 12, 3, 47-52

Stierand, P. (2012) Urbane Landwirtschaft: Was ist das? [Accessed 30 July 2015 at http://speiseraeume.de/faq-urbane-landwirtschaft/]

Taborsky, U. (2008) *Naturzugang als Teil des Guten Lebens: Die Bedeutung interkultureller Gärten in der Gegenwart*. Frankfurt am Main: Lang

Teig, E. Amulya, J., Bardwell, L., Buchenau, M., Marshall, J. and Litt, J. (2009) Collective efficacy in Denver, Colorado: Strengthening neighborhoods and health through community gardens. *Health and Place*, 15,4, 1115-1122

Vahsen, F. G. (2014) *Die erstarrte Gesellschaft: Zum Verlust des Gemeinsinns*. Münster: LIT Verl. (= Soziologie; 86)

Wakefield, S., Yeudall, F., Taron, C., Reynolds, J. And Skinner, A. (2007) *Growing urban health: Community gardening in South-East Toronto. Health Promotion International*, 22, 2, 92-101

Weisbord, M. and S. Janoff (2010) *Future Search: Getting the whole system in the room for vision, commitment, and action*. 3rd ed. San Francisco: Berrett-Koehler

Whiteford, G. and E. Townsend (2011) Participatory occupational justice framework (PJOF 2010): Enabling occupational participation and inclusion, in F. Kronenberg, N. Pollard and D. Sakellariou (Eds.). *Occupational Therapies without Borders. Vol. 2: Towards an ecology of occupation-based practices*. Edinburgh: Churchill Livingstone Elsevier (pp. 65-84)

WHO (World Health Organization) (1986) *Ottawa Charter for Health Promotion* [Accessed 30 July 2015 at http://www.euro.who.int/de/publications/policy-documents/ottawa-charter-for-health-promotion,-1986]

Wilcock, A. A. (2006) *An Occupational Perspective of Health*. 2nd ed. Thorofare NJ: Slack

York, M. and Wiseman, T. (2012) Gardening as an occupation: A critical review. *British Journal of Occupational Therapy*, 75, 2, 76-84

Zinkstok, R. and Schiller, S. (2014) *A Framework to Support Occupational Therapy Students Involved in Projects Based on a Community Development Approach*. Presentation at the 16th World Federation of Occupational Therapists Congress & 48th Japanese Occupational Therapy Congress Yokohama, 19.6.2014

Chapter 4
'We float together:' Immersing occupational therapy students in the Salamander Project

Pamela Karp and Pamela Block

Introduction

In May of 2014, Pamela Block, in collaboration with the Humanities Institute at Stony Brook University, invited Petra Kuppers to present the Salamander Project workshop to students and faculty. The Salamander Project is part of a research series entitled The Olimpias Performance Research Projects (Olimpias, 2015), which explores art with direct audience engagement as a means of fostering social inclusion and highlighting social change and disability culture. Students and faculty from Stony Brook University came together with Kuppers at an indoor swimming pool to experience each other through the free motion of their bodies in the water or by watching and participating from the poolside, as not all participants entered the water. Dry participants serenaded swimmers with poetry readings from selected works that embody the spirit of the project. Swimmers were photographed from an underwater perspective to capture the aesthetic beauty of their bodies as they interacted with one another in the medium and were visually altered by the distorting effects of the water. Following the community performance, the group shared the interpretations and emotional responses that were evoked by the experience.

Most of the students who participated in Kuppers' Salamander Workshop were third year occupational therapy students on the cusp of entering professional practice. Workshop engagement was a requirement for their course, Disabilities Studies and Occupational Therapy. This particular course engages students in learning about cultural and societal influences on experiences, services and opportunities available to disabled people. Typically the course, which Pamela Block has taught annually since 2004, involves a variety of traditional and nontraditional pedagogical experiences involving disability. Students are assigned disability studies readings and films, they may visit community organizations, or scholars and activists may visit the class to give lectures. As emerging health practitioners, students must develop a deep appreciation for disability through a social lens so that they may become effective agents of change capable of empowering the people they will serve throughout their careers.

The Salamander Project challenged the students at first. They were hesitant and unsure of themselves. Those going into the water tentatively entered the pool with furtive glances at their fellow classmates and workshop leaders. Then they began to immerse themselves; both physically and spiritually. Students moved through the water, caringly helped by their fellow participants both in the water and at pool side, as those in the water experienced the soothing sounds of the readings by 'dry' participants. As their bodies were freed in the medium, their minds began to open and allow them, maybe for the first time, to examine their ability to truly consider the lived experience of others and confront their own unconscious biases. Using the students' course journal entries, we discuss how the perceptions of occupational therapy students were moved by their participation in the Salamander Project workshop in such a way that facilitated a deeper understanding not only of themselves, but of those people they will ultimately and intimately interact with as health practitioners. The importance of such changed perceptions is undeniable as it relates to occupation-based practice with individuals, communities, and populations.

The Salamander Project

The Salamander Project was developed by Petra Kuppers and Neil Marcus. Petra is an educator at the University of Michigan, a writer, artist, and dancer. Neil is an internationally recognized playwright, poet, and performer. Through their art they collaborate with each other and a wider community of artists and activists in performances that highlight disability culture, social change, and empowerment. The Salamander Project is just one of their creative endeavors through the Olimpias Project (Olimpias, 2015), an artist's collective charged with bringing together people and engaging them to envision, create, and ultimately become the art. Its projects tend to be participatory - drawing in the audience as a subtle and poetic way of fostering social inclusion. The pieces developed by the Olimpias Collective are poignant and beautiful.

Neil Marcus's spasticity and his boredom with traditional exercise are a challenge for him and Petra to address. In 2013 they began investigating ways in which they might incorporate exercise into Neil's life to help him keep moving. Together, with a few disabled artist friends and an underwater camera, they entered a public pool. What began as a 'self-care project' for Neil to move his stiff limbs became the first artistic interpretations of what is now known as the Salamander Project (Calit2, 2014).

Kuppers describes the Salamander Project as 'ecopoetic work' (Hume, 2013; Kuppers, 2016; Kuppers & Leto, 2012). By this she means that the art is released from traditional boundaries and set free in the environment to fully engage all who participate and all who witness its creation. This community-driven artistic creative process is initiated through exposing groups of people to cultural expressions of disability, embracing the philosophy that embodiments of all sorts evoke beauty and deserve embracing. The images created during the water play, and from the writings derived from the experiences of the participants, are shared through a variety of social media and are readily available on sites such as YouTube and Face book (Salamander Project, 2015). The Salamander Project embodies the spirit of community because of its social inclusion approach to artistic and creative endeavors. How can disabled people participate in fun, creative activities as artists and creators, not just as 'clients' and 'patients' but as artists and creators? What happens when therapeutic engagements are initiated outside of clinical contexts by non-clinicians, indeed initiated and controlled by the disabled people themselves for their own goals and purposes?

Salamander workshops bring this artistic initiative to communities all over the world. They are designed to include swimmers and non-swimmers, wet and dry participants, writers and readers and people of all ages with all types of bodies. Following the water play, the groups gather together, perhaps share a meal, definitely enjoy each other's company as they reflect on the emotions they have evoked and the art they have created together. Kuppers envisions the mythical Salamander as a symbol of transformation, linking the elements of fire and water (Kuppers, 2016; Salamander Project, 2015). As more people participate in the workshops and share their stories, the Salamander Project has blossomed into an artistic creation environmentally rooted in the natural diversity of those who choose to immerse themselves in the experience (Kuppers, 2016; Salamander, 2015).

The occupational therapy program at Stony Brook University

At the time we hosted the Salamander workshop, the occupational therapy program at Stony Brook University offered a program of study leading to a Bachelor's degree in Health Science and a Master's degree in Occupational Therapy. We envision that the ever changing needs of society require practitioners who are academically prepared to address global, community, and individual health concerns. Students in the program are advanced to graduate level status after completing eighteen months of didactic and experiential coursework. At this point, they begin to apply their knowledge in full-time fieldwork experiences and community-based service learning. Students complete thirty-four weeks of fieldwork in a variety of settings and with varied populations.

By the end of the thirty-four weeks of fieldwork, students have undergone a complex transformation. They have interacted with professionals, clients, and families. Their multi-layered experiences in the field have contributed to their growth not only as fledgling occupational therapists, but also as human beings. They return to campus energized and inquisitive about the very nature of the human spirit and ready to engage in their final coursework before graduation. In the course 'Disability and Occupational Therapy,' these students are introduced to social models of disability; they explore the ethical and psychosocial issues faced by disabled people throughout their life span, and develop a rich appreciation and understanding for the complex issues faced by people with disabilities (Block, 2014; Block et al, 2005). The course encompasses, discussions and experiences on disability that vary from year to year. Students might attend lectures, films, or art exhibits. Usually students participate in a disability studies poster session. We also host disability studies scholars and activists in the classroom. The Salamander workshop added an experiential component to the 'Disability and Occupational Therapy' course for the 2014 academic year.

Salamander comes to Stony Brook

In March of 2014, Block began to notify faculty on the Stony Brook Campus that Kuppers was coming to facilitate a Salamander workshop. Students in the Disability and OT course were notified that they would be attending the workshop and would write about the experience as a self-reflection assignment. As emerging health practitioners, students must develop a deep appreciation for disability through a social lens so that they may become effective agents of change capable of empowering the people they will serve throughout their careers. Exposing them to Kuppers' workshop was a step forward in that direction.

What we had not considered was how the pitfalls of life and the timing would influence the experience for both faculty and students. April, just weeks before graduation and the licensing exam, was a very stressful time for the students. April was also when Pamela Block's father entered the final stages of terminal cancer and heart failure. He died just days before the Salamander workshop. Pamela scheduled the shiva (Jewish mourning ritual) so that she could still attend the healing Salamander event.

As we began to organize the participant list, it became clear that students were very hesitant to participate in the workshop. We needed students to agree to go into the pool. At the end of April 2014, we only had three students willing to go into the water and about twenty who wanted to participate without entering the water. Kuppers was honest in her email communications, stating that three in the water with twenty watching would probably be an 'awkward experience' leading those in the water to feel very 'self-conscious'. She asked us to do our best to convince students to enter the pool, stating that it would be a 'beautiful experience'. With much prodding and coaxing we eventually convinced fifteen students to enter the pool while twelve would participate 'dry.' Both Pamela Block and Pamela Karp also entered the pool as 'wet' participants.

Finally, on a warm and rainy day in early May 2014, students and faculty from Stony Brook University came together with Kuppers at an indoor hotel swimming pool to experience each other through the free motion of their bodies in the water. We met Kuppers in the lobby prior to the workshop. It was obvious that Kuppers is an artist and more specifically a dancer. As she entered the lobby to greet us, we were struck by the gracefulness and beauty of her movements. Later, an analogy would be drawn comparing her voice to the water as it flowed just as elegantly in its warmth and invitation. Student participants began to congregate in the lobby. While their eyes shined with eager anticipation, they spoke in hushed, nervous tones. How intriguing! We all moved to the pool deck. While still clothed, Kuppers introduced herself and then requested that each of us do the same. She talked about the Salamander workshop and what she has termed, the 'everyday diversity of the pool' (Kuppers, 2016, p. 38). Kuppers evoked the images of what was to come – bodies coming together in a medium of equality, to congregate, play, and explore not only each other, but also ourselves. As a group we spoke of what we were thankful for and ruminated on what we thought the picture of our lives would include five years forward.

The 'wet' participants entered the water. First they physically supported each other, allowing one another to float atop the hands of their partners. The dry participants recited poetry readings from selected works that embody the spirit of the project. Here are two examples of poems created at one Salamander event, then read at others (Salamander Project, 2015):

Ser Salamandra, ese es la cuestión.
En esta vida hay que poder transformarse, mental y corporalmente.
Bajo el agua todo se transforma.
En el agua el cuerpo recibe impulsos de vida, otra mobilidad, otra manera de danzar

la vida.
(Xavier Duacastilla, Barcelona a 1 de agosto de 2013)

(Being Salamander, that is the question.
In this life you have to be able to transform, mental and bodily.
Underwater everything changes.
In water the body receives life impulses, another mobility, another way of life dancing.
(translated by the author)

Moving in water; light dancing; body dancing.
Movement fluid.
Reflections of his face on the pool's
surface.
He reflects light.
Nose illuminated,
mouth
in shadow.
Play of light
and shadow, water
and body.
Merman exploring, the water
holding him.
Pulsating.
Dancing
in water and light.
Dance reflected
on the surface.
Water movements
fluid. Electricity
provided by the body
and light.
No air bubbles.
The breath is within.
As long as there's breath, remain
in the water.
Then surface
visit.
Humans are bound
to the land, the opposite
of mer-folk.
No gills, no fins. The water is a brief
retreat.
Suspended moment of dance, play,
reflection. Not static,
but bounded.
Light plays by different

rules, bent by water.
Life too.
Bent, twisted,
water dance.
No linear
movements, no straight
lines. Fluid.
The water is a refuge for the offbeat,
the bent,
the other-than-straight. Fluidy
forgives.
The body and mind can remain
fluid as they encounter concrete
streets, impassible
steps, closed
minds.
The dance can
emerge with us, dripping
from the pool
(Beth Currans)

Then the swimmers were photographed from an underwater perspective to capture the aesthetic beauty of their bodies as they interacted with one another and with the water. Following the community performance in the pool, the group then met together to enjoy a meal while they shared their interpretations of the experience and described the emotional responses that were evoked. Student participants had the opportunity at that point to view photographs that were taken of them from below the surface of the water. They were asked to describe and interpret any personal meaning or imagery drawn from the photographs and to do some 'free writes' creative writing inspired by the experience, and some of the students read their free writes out loud to the group and included them in their course journal.

Reflections on the experience: Occupational relevance to participants

Why coax occupational therapy students to participate in a project about spirituality, poetry, imagery? Is there any relevant meaning for them? What would they learn about occupational therapy? What would they learn about themselves? Self-reflections shared with us by the students allowed us to intimately enter their consciousness and understand how the Salamander workshop affected them not only as occupational therapy students, but also as human beings. A number of student participants were hesitant at first. They had been previously exposed to Kuppers' written work, but they had difficulty making sense of what the workshop was supposed to be for them. Their journal entries conveyed a sense of insecurity. This was a situation students had not been previously exposed to in our program. Unlike their didactic coursework, the objectives were not clearly defined and the expectations were not readily apparent. Following two years of organized and structured learning in traditional settings, this free form, artistic endeavor seemed to unsettle our students.

> 'What is Petra Kuppers talking about? What is she going to have us do? To be honest, these were the only questions that came to mind when it came to this week's topic. Reading Petra Kuppers' material before meeting her was confusing for me to fully grasp. I went into the workshop with unsure expectations.'

> 'I was initially hesitant to volunteer to go in the water because I didn't really know what to expect.'

> 'The event at the pool was something I was a bit apprehensive and somewhat confused about when it was first described.'

> 'At first I found the experience a bit confusing, as I was overly concerned with what I was supposed to be doing, what I was supposed to be thinking, what I was supposed to be feeling. Looking around the pool, I think many of my other classmates felt that way as well.'

Some of the writings reflect a desire to frame the workshop in occupational therapy terms that they had already become accustomed to and grown comfortable with.

> 'I reflected on how social activity can play a big role in developing a good quality of life.'

> 'Maybe as therapists, we need to design our therapeutic interventions to be more client-centered so our clients enjoy going to therapy. He [Neil Marcus] may have benefited from aqua therapy.'

Permeating the student reflections is a blossoming of self-awareness and insight that begins to hint at the lessons that will ultimately be brought forth into therapeutic practice.

> 'The Salamander Project allowed participants to . . . let their guards down and create relationships with peers they may not have had prior contact with.'

> 'The exercise we did prior to entering the pool really helped me prepare mentally, and also helped me to reflect and connect with myself—not the person busily living day-to-day, but the real me that was inside.'

> 'By leaning on each other we can develop a mutual relationship.'

> 'I was able to live in the moment and enjoy myself.'

> 'I did not learn any key concepts or terminology, but rather I learned more about myself and felt more in tune with my spiritual self.'

> 'I felt that I was more aware of my surroundings and how important each individual is, whether or not they have a disability... I have to give new people and experiences a chance, in order to grow as an individual.'

Embedded within the students' writings is the foundational structure which will nurture the development of their therapeutic use of self within an occupational justice framework. Noted in the Occupational Therapy Practice Framework (AOTA, 2014, p. s12) as an 'integral part of the occupational therapy process', therapeutic use of self has been defined in many ways throughout the history of occupational therapy.

Contemporary explanations of the therapeutic use of self include key elements such as empathy, trust, and respect as components of a collaborative relationship between the therapist and client. While the use of self remains an integral component in the client-therapeutic relationship, contributing to both verbal and non-verbal communication skills, insight, awareness, openness, and warmth, it can also unconsciously contribute to power imbalances (Mandell, 2008), placing the therapist and client at opposite ends of a socially just continuum. How therapists come to a greater understanding of their clients' narratives relies on their ability to self-evaluate and reflect on their own experiences (Taylor, 2009). How therapists become consciously aware of the social juxtaposition between themselves and their clients requires a critical approach through an occupational justice lens. It is in the personal reflections following the Salamander Workshop that we begin to see sensitivity and self-awareness emerge. These characteristics form the foundation of therapeutic use of self. When therapeutic use of self is supported by an occupational justice framework, students begin to understand the role of social systems as barriers to participation. This then becomes the foundation for socially inclusive practice in which the potential for power disparities in traditional therapeutic relationships is consciously recognized.

Anne Wilcock (2015) has written extensively on the relationship between occupation and health. She notes that the prevailing medical model of health fails to recognize and give credence to the extensive contribution of sociocultural, political, and historical circumstances that affect prevalence, severity and outcome of disease and illness. In discussing how medical practice has influenced occupation, Wilcock (2015, p.71) states that:

> 'when inability to engage in occupations is viewed only from a biologically dysfunctional perspective, it can only be understood as a personal issue and not from the broader perspective as a societal issue.'

Historically, occupational therapists have maintained a fundamental belief in the intimate relationship between occupation and health and the 'centrality of occupation to humanness' (Wilcock, 2015, p. 131). Yet, as the medical model prevails in the world of health services, imparting to students a deep and complex understanding of the holistic interaction between society, health, illness, and occupation continues to be a difficult endeavor. Medically modeled applications are deeply embedded in early didactic coursework to educate students in the evaluation, assessment, and treatment of clients. We came to realize through the students' self reflections following the Salamander workshop that expanding our students' horizons to view health and illness from an occupational perspective was a means of fostering the development of their self-awareness and broader understanding of humans within social contexts and communities.

Conclusion: Lessons for occupational therapy pedagogy

The profession of occupational therapy continues to undergo growth and development to meet the ever increasing complex needs of a changing health services landscape. We have undergone radical changes within our professional education, moving from Bachelors prepared field entry to Masters. By 2025, occupational therapists will require doctoral level preparedness in order to sit for the licensing examination. As our education components have changed and become more complex, our educational philosophies have also been expanded. In 2014, The American Occupational Therapy Association revised their philosophy of education stating that:

> 'Students are… occupational beings in dynamic transaction with the learning context and teaching-learning process. The learning context includes curriculum and pedagogy and conveys a perspective and belief system that includes a view of humans as occupational beings, occupation as a health determinant, and participation as a fundamental right.' (AOTA, 2014, p.2)

The two distinct educational philosophies woven throughout Stony Brook University's occupational therapy program support its vision of nurturing practitioners who embrace and promote the human need to engage in life activities that enhance quality of life. The progressive philosophy of education encourages active participation and engagement in learning and supports commitment to both cultural awareness, ethics, and morality (Little, 2013). Critical thinking and problem solving are tenets in the progressive philosophy which are threaded throughout the curriculum. The Humanist perspective of education facilitates self-actualization within the learner. This holistic philosophy of learning encompasses the importance of 'personal growth, consciousness raising, and empowerment.'(Tangney, 2014, p. 267). The challenge for faculty in our program is to educate future practitioners in the science of occupational therapy and also to nurture their personal development and therapeutic sense of self – all components of self-actualization. We also seek to impart an understanding of the central role of community in occupation, and, as the Salamander Project demonstrates, that health promoting community occupation may takes place quite successfully outside of clinical or therapeutic contexts. In his article on signature pedagogies, Shulman (2005, p.53) noted that 'professional education is not education for understanding alone; it is preparation for accomplished and responsible practice in the service of others.' Shulman aptly states that 'pedagogies that bridge theory and practice are never simple,' (p. 56).

Our third year students who participated in the Salamander Workshop had reached an interesting point along the road of their professional education. Having completed a varied curriculum of didactic coursework and experiential learning in the field, they still needed a nurturing of their professional souls. Magalhães (2012) fears that an occupational therapy ever in pursuit of science leads us to 'embrace a soul-less discipline,' (p.12) and that 'somehow we have been able to sanitize our work so that it is free of such contentious topics as *hope* and *love*,' (original emphasis p. 16). This being the 'occupational therapy soul' from which our students' moral values and integrity would become more clearly defined and understood within the context of professional life, we need to take conscious action as teachers to counter-act this sanitized view of life and practice. The role our students might ultimately play in enhancing community and social inclusion is still developing. How can we try to ensure it grows in ways that encourage collective responsibility for wellbeing?

There is extensive literature on pedagogy as it applies to problem-based and experiential learning within the health professions. Our curriculum incorporates didactic and experiential learning opportunities to facilitate clinical reasoning and problem solving skills in our students. However, in order to meet our obligation to also facilitate our students' full potential as occupational therapists, we, as faculty, must look beyond the borders of current traditional methodologies to expand our students self reflective abilities and nurture what will ultimately become their occupational consciousness or what Magalhães might call their professional soul. Kronenberg, Pollard, and Ramugondo (2011) have described occupational consciousness as an awareness and appreciation of the role of personal and collective occupations which perpetuate practices that foster cultural power of dominant groups over others. To aid in the development of occupational consciousness, we understood the need, as occupational therapy educators, to nurture an understanding of occupational justice concepts. How can students learn to examine the issues of social justice, namely inequality, unfairness, and discrimination, from an occupational perspective?

In her powerful discourse on the need to transform the clinical relationship between 'powerful experts' and 'sick people,' (Pillay, 2011) offers an imbalance of power view that may erringly be fostered within all occupational therapy programs. As health practitioners, we engage in methods that 'build biologic images of patients through a medical gaze' (p.124). We have come to the understanding that we must create and offer learning experiences that foster an awareness of the need for change in ideologies that clearly separate and unequally position rehabilitation professionals and people with disabilities. This awareness is an essential step toward self-actualization and our students' critical awareness of their developing sense of therapeutic self. Even to the point of understanding how 'therapeutic self' might sometimes maintain power inequalities within professional relationships and the need to value creative health promotion strategies, such as the Salamander Project, that originate from outside the clinical context. Bringing Kuppers to our campus to challenge ingrained assumptions about society and placing the students in the uncomfortable position of facing their own culturally manufactured biases about the juxtaposition of their roles as health professionals and people with disabilities became a valuable lesson, not just to the students, but also to us as educators. We learned that providing culturally artistic experiences outside of the traditional classroom and clinic offered our students a unique and engaging opportunity to examine with a greater perspective what it means to live life to the fullest, not only for their potential collaborations in future therapeutic and community partnerships, but for themselves as well. The evidence of our students burgeoning occupational consciousness is revealed in their self -reflections.

The workshop demonstrated '...the importance of unity amongst all participants'. 'Being able to understand and accept those around you is a concept we can relate directly to working with those who have a disability.'

Insight was evident through this student's self-reflection:

'While in the water, I experienced support from my partner as well as from the individuals outside of the water. This showed how there can be interdependence and interconnectedness from the disabled and able-bodied population.'

Occupational conscious is highlighted in this reflection: 'We need to form a partnership with our clients to attain the greatest results rather than exerting authority over our clients.'

The Salamander Workshop experience provided us, as educators, an avenue for further student development in a manner that differs from traditional teaching models. Shulman (2005, p.52) describes signature pedagogies as 'characteristic forms of teaching and learning.' When we envision the signature pedagogy of occupational therapy education, our learning models are replete with lectures, lab experiences, and case studies. Our students are involved in community-based projects which also serve to enhance the learning experience. As faculty we feel the weight of responsibility for the education of our future practitioners. We want them to not only be knowledgeable in their areas of practice, not only to be able to reason clinically, but we wish to instill in them a deeper appreciation for human beings and the social contexts in which individuals and communities find meaning and joy, hope and love, in their occupations and their lives. This can only be done in collaboration and alliance with the communities we wish to support.

The Salamander Workshop gave us one opportunity to test the waters of a complementary learning model intended to help students more fully immerse themselves in the lived experience of others. In doing so here and in other community-based experiences seeded throughout our curriculum, we hope that as they grow into practitioners of occupational therapy, our students will develop an increased ability to view the experiences of others through an occupational justice lens, and an understanding of the social contexts in which they will practice.

Acknowledgements

The authors would like to thank Petra Kuppers for bringing Salamander to Stony Brook University and for all her supportive comments and suggestions for various drafts of this chapter. We also want to thank the Stony Brook University Occupational Therapy Class of 2014 for their bravery, openness and creativity. Thanks also to the Humanities Institute at Stony Brook University for sponsoring Petra's visit to Stony Brook University in May 2014. Thanks to Bradley Karat and Rebecca DePasquale for their copy-editing assistance.

References

American Occupational Therapy Association (2014) Occupational therapy practice framework: Domain and process 3rd ed. *American Journal of Occupational Therapy*, 68, s1, s2-s51

American Occupational Therapy Association (2007) Philosophy of occupational therapy education. *American Journal of Occupational Therapy*, 61, 6, 678

Block, P., Ricafrente-Biazon, M., Russo, A., Chu, K.Y., Sud, S., Koerner, L., Vittoria, K., Langrover, A. and Olowu, T. (2005) Introducing disability studies to occupational therapy students. Special Issue on Occupational Therapy and Disability Studies, *American Journal of Occupational Therapy*, 59, 4, 554-60

Block, P. (2014) *Course syllabus for Disability and Occupational Therapy HAO 585.* Stony

Brook University

Calit2. (2014) *The Salamander Project: Disability Culture Art/Life* [video file] [Accessed 3 February 2015 at https://www.youtube.com/watch?v=iJ6G-rtZqck]

Hume, A. (2013) *Queering ecopoetics: Nonnormativity, (anti)futurity, precarity.* Field Notes from the 2013 Conference on Ecopoetics. [Accessed December 21 2015 at http://jacket2. org/commentary/queering-ecopoetics-nonnormativity-antifuturity-precarity]

Kronenberg, F., Pollard, N. and Ramugondo, E. (2011) Introduction: courage to dance politics. in F. Kronenberg, N. Pollard and D. Sakellariou (Eds.) *Occupational Therapy Without Borders, vol. 2: Towards an ecology of occupation-based practices.* NY: Churchill Livingston Elsevier (pp. 1-16)

Kuppers, P. (2016) Swimming with the Salamander: A community eco-performance project. *Performing Ethos,* 5 ,1&2), 33-49

Kuppers P, and Leto, D. (2012) A Radiant Approaching. [Accessed 21 December 2015 at https://www.youtube.com/watch?v=WihPJuFaBNg]

Little, T. (2013) 21st century learning and progressive education: An intersection. *International Journal of Progressive Education,* 9, 1, 84-96

Magalhães, L. (2012) What would Paulo Freire think of occupational science? in G.E. Whiteford and C. Hocking (Eds.) *Occupational Science: Society, inclusion, participation.* Chichester: Wiley-Blackwell (pp 8-19)

Mandell, D. (2008) Power, care and vulnerability: Considering use of self in child welfare work. *Journal of Social Welfare Practice,* 22, 2, 235-248

Olimpias (2015) *The Olimpias Performance Research Projects.* [Accessed 21 December 2015 at http://www-personal.umich.edu/~petra/]

Pillay, M. (2011) (Re)habilitation and (re)positioning the powerful expert and the sick person. in F. Kronenberg, N. Pollard and D. Sakellariou (Eds.) *Occupational Therapy Without Borders, vol. 2: Towards an ecology of occupation-based practices.* NY: Churchill Livingston Elsevier (pp. 123-141)

Salamander Project (2015) *Salamander Project Description.* [Accessed 21 December 2015 at http://www-personal.umich.edu/~petra/salamander.html]

Shulman, L.S. (2005) Signature pedagogies on the professions. *Daedalus,* 134, 3, 52-59.

Tangney, S. (2014) Student-centred learning: A humanist perspective. *Teaching in Higher Education,* 19, 3, 266-275

Taylor, R.R., Lee, S.W., Kielhofner, G. and Ketkar, M. (2009) Therapeutic use of self: A nationwide survey of practitioners' attitudes and experiences. *American Journal of Occupational Therapy,* 63, 2, 198-207

Wilcock, A. (2015) *An occupational perspective of health.* Thorofare, NJ: Slack

Image 1. Petra Kuppers and Sunaura Taylor drive under the water together. Petra's arm is around Sunaura's shoulders, supporting and guiding her. Their eyes are closed and bubbles flow from Sunaura's mouth and from her kicking legs. The walls of the pool are dark brown, in contrast to the bright light streaming down the backs of the swimmers.

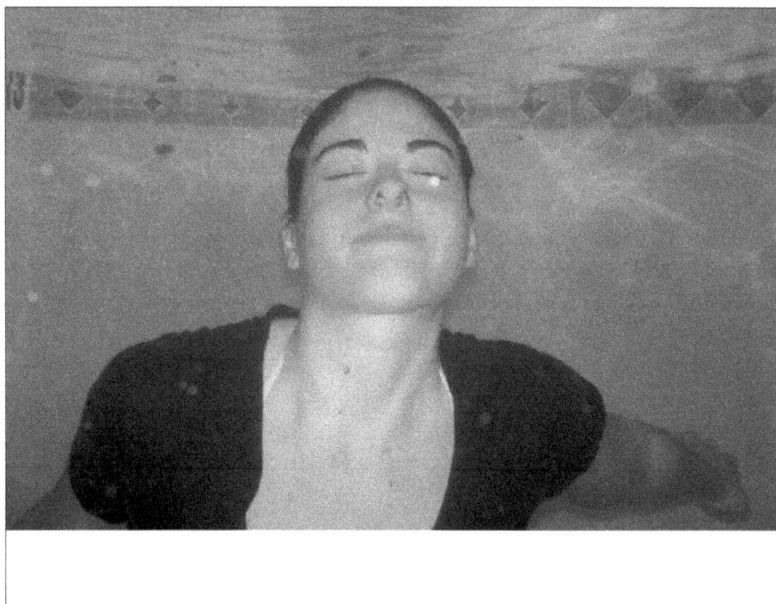

Image 2. Occupational therapy student Samantha Truono smiles contentedly from the bottom of the pool. Her eyes are closed.

Image 3. Petra Kuppers is supporting Pamela Block's body in the water with her arms and hands.

Image 4. Sandy Chung, OTS a dark haired Asian woman with hair pulled back, meditates peacefully under water - eyes closed, fingers in a loosely held chakra position. Her finger nails are different shades of blue and bubbles rise from her nose.

Image 5. Elizabeth Hemmings, OTS with her eyes wide open and her hair loose and flowing around her face. One hand, palm facing the camera, fingers splayed.

Chapter 5
Engaging with service users

Jacqui McKenna, Steven Roberts and Ellen Tickle

Introduction

This chapter explores the engagement of service users in the design of the BSc (Hons) degree curriculum at the University of Salford (UK), and within this context it discusses the perceptions, opinions and experiences of those service users, regarding the perceived importance of engagement in therapy and the application of related skills, knowledge and attitudes by the occupational therapist.

Occupational therapy is underrepresented in the literature regarding service user involvement in curriculum design (Morgan & Jones, 2009). The service user voice in shaping health care education is becoming increasingly more important with the evidence base discussing a range of benefits (Bourdreau et al, 2008; Repper & Breeze, 2007). Service users include disenfranchised communities (Ocloo & Fulop, 2010) and the broader demands of these groups vary and include citizenship issues, welfare rights, challenging societal attitudes and barriers and the entitlement to be involved in decisions impacting upon them, leading to greater expectations of service providers and society (Chambers & Hickey, 2012).

Service user members of our curriculum design team identified that one of the biggest potential barriers to building a successful relationship with their therapist and engaging in the therapeutic process, was the occupational therapist themselves. They identified that their need to be listened to and understood, whilst engaged in an efficacious therapeutic alliance (regardless of the wider systems or contexts of practice), was vital. Curriculum change is an important vehicle in supporting the currency and relevance of education and our curriculum developments specifically addressed the knowledge, skills and attitudes necessary to work toward engagement which supports occupational participation; thus providing an educational strategy which ultimately supports social inclusion.

Background

Educational and professional drivers

The BSc (Hons) Occupational Therapy programme was established in 1998 and is subject to quinquennial institutional review. To ensure teaching and learning standards were met, currency maintained and the relevance of the curriculum continued to lead to graduates fit for purpose and professional practice, professional and regulatory body guidelines were consulted during the review process. These included: Health and Care Professions Council (HCPC) Standards of Proficiency (2013) and Standards of

Education and Training (2014); Royal College of Occupational Therapists (RCOT) Learning and Development Standards for Pre-Registration Education (2014) and Code of Ethics and Professional Conduct (2010). Whilst professional and regulatory body guidelines have subsequently been updated this module continues to meet requirements for curriculum development and professional standards and was reapproved in accordance with current procedures in 2019, supporting concurrency and regulatory compliance (RCOT, 2019)

The Francis Report (2013) made recommendations for health care provision and the competencies of health care staff, with implications for the pre-registration education and training of all health care professionals, with the specific goal of producing staff able to provide compassionate care. Additionally, ensuring newly qualified occupational therapists are equipped with the knowledge and skills to cope with the demands of the real work environment is imperative, necessitating that the political agenda is connected to the occupational therapy role. Practice is informed by political awareness and exposing the therapist to a more diverse spectrum of world views (Pollard et al., 2008), would enable them to be responsive to change and embrace emerging roles and practices.

Working collaboratively with service users to design and deliver student training and education is a key issue, with the guidelines of HCPC (2014; 2012), RCOT (2014) and the Department of Health (DOH 2013; 2009) recommending these partnerships. Given that service users have long identified the importance of their involvement, whilst also demonstrating a willingness to engage (Speers, 2008), capturing service user opinion and meaningfully involving them in curriculum development was considered essential.

The key themes generated during our discussions with service users, alongside professional body requirements and standards (HCPC, 2014; RCOT, 2014), were utilised to develop learning outcomes for the BSc (Hons) Occupational Therapy programme, and specifically for the module, 'Engaging Service Users in Occupational Therapy' (ESUOT). Our educational strategy within the ESUOT module recognises service users as experts in their own lives and in terms of their experiences of the therapeutic relationship and engagement in occupational therapy, challenging the professionals' belief that they are or should be all knowing. All experience is constructed through the lens of the subjective individual and it is this which must be captured in order to meaningfully inform the perspective explored by students.

Social inclusion, occupational participation and occupational therapy

Social inclusion involves reducing inequality, increasing integration into society, facilitating engagement in valued roles, encouraging achievement of potential and control thereby promoting wellbeing (Harrison & Sellers, 2008; Britton & Casebourne, 2002). It cannot be assumed that social inclusion is desirable or supportive of health if it is not the service users' choice (LeBoutillier & Croucher, 2010). Morris (2001) explores the tendency for social inclusion policy to problematise the individual. A society reluctant to include people with disabilities is the root of the problem and therefore attitudinal change rather than an individual focus, is essential in order to support social inclusion.

Service users discussed the value of a committed therapist who will fight for what you need, but would not expect therapists to 'get into trouble'. Maybe trouble is exactly what we should be causing in order to ensure we are a profession wherein service user centeredness reflects practice rather than good intentions or rhetoric (Hammell, 2007) and therapists at the forefront of socially inclusive practice work to avoid the perpetuation of disabling ideology (Weinberg, 2015; Harrison & Sellers, 2008). A more inclusive approach to practice necessitates an exploration of the limited perspectives of holism held within the profession (Couldrick, 2005), and must acknowledge the risks health and social care interventions may pose in terms of deprivation of power, choice and opportunity when resources are restricted. The privilege of our position is inherent and linked to our professional status and according to Weinberg (2015) power is drawn from acting upon this privilege. Whilst we claim to be client centered, a term which in itself carries inherent assumptions, it is the professional who defines what constitutes health and dysfunction, determining what service is appropriate to be provided in order to address any issues, highlighting the power differential and inevitably impacting the authenticity of any relationship.

Occupational participation plays a central role in achieving social inclusion and facilitating engagement in occupations will support the sustainable inclusion of both individuals and groups in society (LeBoutillier & Croucher, 2010). An authentic alliance underpinned by presence and commitment facilitates co-participation and the application of occupational reasoning (Tickle-Degnen, 2014; Taylor, 2008), supporting participation. Empowering individuals, groups and communities, with and without disabilities, to participate in occupations is the vital contribution made by the occupational therapist (Reed et al, 2011; Harrison & Sellers, 2008). Individuals are deserving of emotional connection, flexibility, personal control and actualisation (Taylor, 2008). Service user centred practice necessitates an understanding of the meaning, demands and context of occupations for the individual and is so much more than simply 'doing' (Hocking, 2009), as it is concerned with the subjective experience of the individual and their ability to orchestrate their everyday occupations by making choices about what, when, where and with whom activities are done (Wilcock, 2006). 'An effective therapist shapes lives' (Zinker, 1977, p.37), we must approach this role with the passion, respect and humility it deserves, recognising the privilege of our position, the art of our practice and the limitless potential at our fingertips.

Poor engagement is a significant barrier to participation in occupation, potentially impacting social inclusion. This necessitates that the therapist and service user engage both with each other and with the occupation, utilising effective engagement skills and strategies in order to prevent social exclusion. The education of undergraduates should ensure there is not only an understanding of the risks and consequences of individuals and groups becoming socially excluded, but also that students develop the skills and strategies needed to support engagement.

Engagement

Engagement is complex, subjective and multifaceted, viewed both as a construct and as an observable entity. It is often used interchangeably with participation and can be defined as a commitment to working toward goals of therapy, or a deliberate effort to actively participate and be involved in occupations (Lequerica et al., 2009). As service user involvement in the programme expands, we anticipate that a more focused definition and view of engagement in the occupational therapy setting will be developed and utilised to refine curriculum planning.

An important feature of engagement is the relationship between the therapist and service user. Overwhelmingly, service user opinion suggested that communication, commitment, presence and emotion management were most important in developing the collaborative relationship.

'Having knowledge and skills in terms of occupational therapy treatments and such is valuable, but if they can't connect, it's pointless.'

Knowledge and skill application can only be useful when applied to meet the needs of the individual, group or community and is based upon the foundation of sound and effective engagement from the start of the occupational therapy process. Engagement requires commitment, flexibility and adaptation and is dependent upon connection to an individual, group or community's priorities and needs (McKenna, 2007). Reid (2009) linked this connection to mutual presence in an activity, which is both effective and satisfying facilitating improved experience, outcomes and satisfaction for all participants (Wright & Stickley, 2015; Tickle-Degnen, 2014; Weng et al, 2011). McKenna (2016) states that the ability to maximise the therapeutic alliance positively impacts upon occupational engagement, facilitating shared goals and a sense of belonging and identity, suggesting that engagement and satisfaction are linked to emotional wellbeing for participants as a sense of purpose, achievement and self-efficacy are developed. In order to challenge disabling ideology the occupational therapist should imbue inclusive principles within their practice and apply these to every interaction, engaging service users in partnerships which facilitate occupational participation and support wellbeing and full participation in society.

The Process: Service user members of the curriculum development team

Despite political and professional drivers, service user involvement in curriculum development is not widespread (Higgins et al, 2011), and we wanted to innovate and achieve true, collaborative curriculum design at the University of Salford. We wanted to look, think and act, working in coalition with service users in our process. A strategy of service user involvement is in place in the University of Salford and as advised by the Social Care Institute for Excellence (2007), a participatory culture within the organisation is more likely to support participation.

The occupational therapy programme has a history of collaborative working with stakeholders, establishing working relationships with service users who regularly contribute to the delivery of the curriculum. We wanted our experience of curriculum design to be inclusive, facilitating shared learning and supporting the generation of new knowledge which could be applied to the curriculum. The working team were involved in the whole process, influencing the development of the process itself, within the limits of the professional and educational context. The project is part of a longitudinal process, involving service users from different perspectives and experiences to refine and focus curriculum change, allowing engagement and its importance to evolve, supporting the application of theoretical and practical strategies.

Sixteen service users have worked with us for an average of four years, although some partnerships have been established for longer and have been drawn from a variety of sources. All the service users have had contact with a range of statutory, private, charitable and voluntary sector provision or projects. Alongside more traditional services, users have engaged with advocacy projects, social enterprises and cooperatives, community wellbeing centres, service user run support and activity initiatives. Two service users are currently employed in disability awareness roles, one has held chairmanship of a large disability organisation, two have held advocacy roles with local charities and one is currently managing a service user led community gardening enterprise, facilitating us to explore broader perspectives outside of the professional one. All have had involvement with health care professionals including occupational therapists, as both service users and/or colleagues, some more recently than others and all have lived or are living with a range of health issues, physical and/ or mental, and/or issues with their occupations.

The service users were informed of the review, its purpose and our intent to work collaboratively to develop a new curriculum. An initial briefing addressed the objective aspects of this process of inclusion (ELSiTO, 2015) and information provided was distilled to mediate both information overload and any power differential, which at this stage was evident and unavoidable as staff had system and process expertise. Subsequently fourteen service users agreed to participate with one being unable to commit due to ill health. The subjective aspects of inclusion began to evolve as engagement in the process was facilitated, negotiating roles and the expectations of participation. Shared goals were established and the group contextualised their engagement in an activity with purpose and value by working in the University environment. Service users were offered payment for their contributions to curriculum development and have commented that payment supports perception of them as the providers of expertise which is worthy of purchase. Applying this principle to this activity supported the management of the power imbalance by identifying service users and staff as paid members of a team of experts. Evidence supports that service users develop increased self-worth, confidence and empowerment, derived from the acknowledgement of their expertise (Rhodes et al, 2013; Tee, 2012). Service user experiences of involvement were positive with no negative effects reported, discussion of perceived benefits included being valued and engaging in a meaningful and purposeful occupation (Morgan & Jones, 2009). It was vital to ensure service users felt their skills and experiences were of value, and their contribution was not merely tokenistic (McKeown et al, 2014; Branfield, 2009).

We wanted to support participation of all team members by imbuing a sense of purpose, belonging, trust and shared responsibility. This required the team to address early on in the process, key issues surrounding the expertise held within the group with regard to both the Higher Education system and the requirements of the validating body. Group discussions proved interesting, raising awareness for service users of the staff members differing experience and expertise and challenging perceptions that all staff had expertise in a specific area. The process 'expert' was identified as the programme leader (PL), who agreed to advise the group on the Higher Education system and process, whilst monitoring alignment with professional body requirements. Challenges encountered during the process included: time and process demands, training needs for staff and service users, demands on staff time and variance in use of communication technology. The realities of working to a non-negotiable University deadline led to time pressure and workload related stress for staff. Some staff became frustrated with the amount of discussion around terminology in learning outcomes, which for staff is expected, understood and obviously linked to taxonomy. Whilst helpful in terms of service user understanding, explaining the taxonomy served to widen the power imbalance as it highlighted the use of educational language by the staff. Whilst the use of an incremental approach may assist with gradual cultural adjustment and readiness (Morgan & Jones, 2009), it was not possible to build additional time resources into this process of programme approval. This would need to be considered more carefully for the next approval cycle.

It became clear that service users also had expertise and knowledge and staff had to assimilate this understanding into the context of service users leading the process; academics felt their role and credibility was being challenged which could present barriers to having a partnership or alliance. When service users are engaged as experts, staff need to accept them as experts and must be prepared to discuss and manage their own responses to perceived threats to their own expertise (Branfield, 2009). Despite our efforts to encourage free expression service users' may have felt being asked to evaluate and comment on those professionals who were asking them to engage in this consultation was difficult. Within an educational setting, a true alliance with service users could be questioned as their inclusion is under the control of the institution, serving its purposes, rather than that of the service users (Schon, 2016), and with decisions regarding how and where service users are to be involved being controlled by professionals (Cowden & Singh, 2007, Felton & Stickley, 2004). Redressing the power imbalance remains challenging, as cultural barriers to successfully achieving this were in operation within the educational institution.

Existing relationships were utilised to facilitate an inclusive communication approach which supported members of the working team to explore and negotiate decisions, roles and responsibilities. This approach maximised trust, collaboration and the equalisation of power, reducing any barriers to acceptance of service user credibility and expertise (Branfield, 2009; Felton & Stickley, 2004).

Reflective discussion was used throughout the process and the team identified that important learnings could be drawn from an exploration of what service users felt makes a 'good' occupational therapist. Focus groups were used to explore this question and were facilitated by staff members of the curriculum development team known to the service users. Open questions explored specific areas which included: essential knowledge and skills (interpersonal skills); attitudes and approach; the therapeutic relationship; engagement and experiences of both a poor and good occupational therapy experience. Member checking confirmed scribed notes and thematic analysis captured and summarised data generated, distillation of data generated emergent themes. This qualitative data offered rich, subjective insights and whilst generalisability is not claimed the emergent themes aligned generally with the literature. The findings were used to inform development of programme learning outcomes and content of a newly designed module 'Engaging Service Users in Occupational Therapy' (ESUOT). The learning outcomes were generated using emergent themes, the literature, and professional body requirements which were mapped by the group using a colour coding system, enabling us to synthesise our understandings and reach broad consensus. The service user focus group brought out varied yet equally important strands for consideration and the multidimensional nature of engagement in the occupational therapy setting was highlighted by the involvement of service users with different lived experiences.

The findings: Key emergent themes

The service users had a range of opinions and experiences of the occupational therapy process and they identified engagement as the most important issue. Summarising their comments leads us to define engagement as a connection or involvement with the occupational therapist, with the occupation and with the intervention process. The factors that have supported or obstructed their engagement were discussed and these included: the therapeutic relationship; connection and partnership between service user and therapist; the occupational therapists' knowledge and skills; communication; the therapists' involvement and availability and the management of emotions. Emergent themes will be now discussed within the context of occupational therapy practice and verbatim service user quotes have been included for illustrative purposes.

Engagement and the therapeutic relationship

'There's no point knowing anything if you can't communicate, engage me, and then use it.'

Whilst service users acknowledged the value of knowledge and skills they asserted that the therapeutic relationship was of more importance in enabling participation and engaging them in occupational therapy. An authentic relationship requires presence, attendance, genuineness, empathy and emotion management (Tickle-Degnen, 2014; McKenna & Mellson, 2013). A balance of attitudes, skills and values will support development of an intentional relationship which enables individuals to achieve health and wellbeing through occupational engagement (Weinstein, 2013; McKenna, 2010). Service users confirmed that meaningful and respectful relationships supported their participation, and that trusting the therapist and being engaged by them, meant that they could overcome uncertainty or resistance early in the process. The use of unique abilities and characteristics of both therapist and service user as tools within the relationship can enable engagement and participation. A positive, genuine, flexible and resourceful therapist will engender the trust and motivation necessary for challenging interaction and creative problem solving (Weinstein, 2013; Sumsion, 2006; Rosa & Hasselkus, 2005).

Engagement in a collaborative alliance with the therapist will support engagement in the process of occupational therapy and in the occupation itself. Engagement in occupation necessitates capturing service user motivation and requires an understanding of purpose, meaning and passion (Polatajko, 2014). Passion is reflected in an affinity with an activity and the value of passion as a motivator for participation is essential to the engagement process (Mullen et al, 2011).

Capturing service user perceptions and experiences of wellbeing is influential in the decisions they make about participation in occupations. Links made by service users to personal goal achievement, connectedness, belonging and community involvement are key factors in their engagement (McMaham & Estes, 2011; Hayword & Taylor, 2011). This is summarised clearly by service user opinion below:

'Know me well enough, how to help me achieve, keep me engaged in the plan.'

The service user group identified the consequences of limited engagement as: poor connection and collaboration, reduced motivation and activity, limited goal achievement and satisfaction, poor perceptions of self-efficacy and productivity, exclusion or limited participation in society. Engagement does not only refer to the service user and poor engagement of the therapist in the process puts them at risk of increased stress and a reduction in satisfaction, confidence, capability perception, effectiveness and motivation (Weng et al, 2011; Brackett et al, 2011; Boylan & Loughrey, 2007). If the process of engagement can be broken down into component parts and required knowledge and skills and attitudes identified, then arguably it can be taught in order to support competency and in generating learning outcomes for the ESUOT module this was the approach utilised.

In practice service users commented that connections are difficult to make if they feel the therapist 'doesn't get them or can't relate'. The assumption that western theoretical models and approaches meet the needs of all service users presents a risk of exclusion and the therapist needs compassion, good self-awareness and political attunement to address related issues.

Occupational therapists need to examine the veracity of their claims of altruism, with disability theorists and service users suggesting that the ethical implications of serving both service user and employer challenges service user centered care significantly (Pollard et al, 2008; Hammell, 2007). The demands made by any established institution within which therapists work and the therapists reinforcement of disabling practice, procedure or attitude, can subvert service user centered practice. Classroom activities which critically address the political agenda, making stronger links with disability groups and involving them in programme delivery, will support increased political awareness for students. Utilising service user narratives and experiences within the ESUOT module will allow students to explore the real world challenges of service user centeredness and the building of therapeutic relationships within this context.

The occupational therapists 'toolkit' (knowledge and skills)

'Knowledgeable and able to use that…… adapt it to fit my needs.'

The service users described the professional knowledge and skills essential for the competent occupational therapist as a 'toolkit'. The competent therapist must maintain knowledge and technical skills and the interdependence between knowledge and its application is recognised by the service users as a necessary element of effective occupational therapy practice. However, the overriding issue raised here was that expertise is of little use without an ability to engage the service user early on, linking effective knowledge application to a concurrent and commensurate caring attitude. As the education of health care professionals in the UK has moved rapidly toward degree exit awards, the debate around caring skills versus technical and academic expertise has grown with Bee et al. (2008) suggesting that professions have focused on technical and academic skills at the expense of service user centred care and compassion. Studies have found that service users prioritised softer skills and attitudes including empathy, communication, caring and individualised approach (Griffiths et al, 2012; Bee et al, 2008). The application of skills and knowledge is also dependent upon the therapist having clarity and confidence about their own expertise, role and purpose (Griffiths et al., 2012), and being able to communicate this clearly;

'They need to understand what an OT can do here, what is available, and make sure I understand too'.

Service user perception and experience is as essential in achieving engagement, understanding, autonomy and the generation of shared goals, as the therapists' information, knowledge and skills.

Disability groups advocate for an approach based on applied clinical information or expertise being made relevant by the therapist's awareness and understanding of the specific, subjective lived experience of the individual service user (ReTHINK. org 2015; UK Stroke forum, 2015). It is vital that the interdependence of clinical and personal perspectives is reinforced within the education of students. The ESUOT module will apply this approach by including lived experiences as a focus for classroom activity which is co-facilitated by the service users and staff, equipping students with the knowledge and skills to support their future practice.

Important issues around the relationship and the development of engagement

Service users identified the value of good communication, presence and emotion management as essential for engagement.

Communication

'Talk to me like an ordinary person.'

Effective communication is an essential skill that supports holistic practice (RCOT, 2010), and is the most important skill in every field of occupational therapy practice (Adam et al, 2013). Efficacious communication requires mastery of a range of skills and application of essential attitudes and attributes, which when applied well results in mutual satisfaction and a shared experience of responsiveness, positivity, motivation, connectedness and progress which supports engagement.

'Listen and build a good relationship.'

Listening and questioning skills are cited as essential by the service users as they support real understanding of the individual, validating their experience and self-worth (Griffiths et al., 2012). Evidence supports that there are seven pathways through which therapist communication can positively impact health,

'Increased access to care, knowledge, shared understanding, higher quality medical decisions, enhanced therapeutic alliances, increased social support, empowerment and better management of emotions' (Street et al, 2009, p.295).

Presence, mindfulness and flow

'Really knowing we are working together, they understand me and are in there with me working on it.'

Presence theory explains the focusing of energy, looking, listening, thinking, feeling and learning in order to connect with other people (Rodenberg, 2009). Being mindfully present requires being in that space and moment, active, aware, available and connected (Reid, 2009; Senge et al, 2004). Presence influences how you engage with others and enable their participation, essential for development of a therapeutic relationship as it supports development of trust and collaborative working. Being present is a demonstration of commitment to the service user, the therapeutic alliance and the activity and is linked to empathy and authenticity (Yerxa, 2011), facilitating attuned, respectful and sensitive practice. There are clear links between presence and the concept of flow (Csikszentmihalyi, 1990), which describes the relationship between perceptions of current challenge and available resource, with optimal flow occurring when there is a perceived balance between demand and available skills. In order to remain in flow it is vital to engage in new challenges, to stretch, improve, reach potential and be productive (Csikszentmihalyi, 1990). Applying principles of productivity and purpose aligns with the tenets of our profession and those of social inclusion, leading us back to consider the effective engagement of the service user and their participation in meaningful and productive occupations. The experience of flow depends upon the service users' subjective view of challenges, goals and resources. Being truly present supports the necessary connection, understanding of demand and resource and the shared goals essential for effective engagement by the occupational therapist.

Successful engagement requires that the occupational therapist is present and free from any distractions and barriers that may negatively impact upon the development of the connection. The difficulties this presents in a demanding, modern workplace are clear.

'I also learnt the power of being present in a given situation. It facilitated communication, but it also enabled a shared understanding.'

Emotional Intelligence

'The OT has to get how I feel and know what to do with that, know how they feel about how I feel, so the emotions don't get in the way, and we can get on with what we need to do.'

Bailey et al. (2011) support the belief that the single most important factor in superior performance and effectiveness for healthcare professionals is emotional intelligence (EI). Mayer and Salovey (1997) describe EI as the understanding, perception, use and management of emotions of both self and others. EI skills mediate emotional labour and support development of professional and therapeutic relationships, fostering the application of person-centred, holistic principles (Petrovici & Dobrescu, 2014; McKenna, 2007). Service users highlighted the importance of an emotional connection with the therapist in the process of successful engagement (Cherry et al, 2014; Suhaimi et al, 2014). An emotionally intelligent occupational therapist will understand and manage the emotions of self and others, be warm, genuine, optimistic and persistent, fostering the application of person-centred principles, enhancing both the relationship and therapeutic progress.

'Emotionally sound, - I need to rely on them.'
The occupational therapist's ability to understand, mediate and manage the emotions of self and others undoubtedly impacts on their effectiveness (McKenna & Mellson, 2013; Mayer & Cobb, 2000), and on their ability to engage with service users, carers and communities.

The competent occupational therapist balances the demands of their role effectively and EI abilities support the awareness and management of self and others. EI can be developed using targeted educational interventions which assist in the development of skills and knowledge that support emotional awareness and the development of relationship building skills and coping mechanisms, supporting staff with the emotional demands of service provision (Cherry et al, 2014; Bailey et al, 2011).

Outcomes and actions

A number of outcomes and actions have led from this process of service user involvement in the development of our curriculum.

- The Directorate of Occupational Therapy at the University has service user representatives sitting on the Strategic Advisory Group, involving them directly in curriculum planning more fully than has previously occurred. Service user experts contribute to the delivery and assessment of programme modules and are engaged in admission and selection processes.
- The authors have explored service user experience and embraced their expertise within a process of knowledge generation and translation (Straus et al, 2009), applying learnings to shape the development of the BSc (Hons) Occupational Therapy curriculum at the University.
- Experiences of occupational therapy were explored in order to inform collaborative generation of learning outcomes for both the BSc (Hons) programme and the ESUOT module with learning outcomes informed by the evidence base and our synthesised understandings. The module develops the knowledge and skills required for effective engagement of individuals, groups and communities in collaborative relationships and in occupations, and will be delivered by a range of service users, tutors and engagement experts from outside the profession. Early student feedback on module content indicates that it is of value for both professional and personal development.
- The research team will evaluate the ESUOT module and its impact in a number of ways including student experiential reflections, use of a subjective measure of perceived self-efficacy and pre and post module delivery, measures of trait

emotional intelligence and empathy.

- The service users involved were largely self-selecting and this could suggest that we accessed already proactive service users perpetuating exclusion of those less active. We will seek to include disability groups or members of the disability community who are not currently engaged with the University. This will broaden the range of service user organisations that input to delivery of the programme and specifically to the ESUOT module and strengthening awareness of the political agenda by making more formal links with service user organisations.
- Service users will continue to inform and shape curriculum content, and the changing needs of service users from a wide ranging background will offer further insights with which to strengthen professional understanding of engagement.
- Further exploration of the staff perspective will offer insights to inform our service user involvement strategy.
- Regardless of the developing wider context of our practice, occupational therapists require the skills necessary to communicate, negotiate, connect and engage others in order to enable others and themselves to do more of what matters to them.

Acknowledgements

Thanks to: John, Chris, Paul, Ryan, Daniel, Nadine, Vincent, Mike, Roy, Gill, David and those not wanting to appear by name, for their willingness to engage, share wisdom and participate in our journey of learning and development with enthusiasm and commitment.

References

Adam, K., Peters, S. and Chipchase, L. (2013) Knowledge skills and professional behaviours required by occupational therapist and physiotherapist beginning practitioners in work related practice: A systematic review. *Australian Occupational Therapy Journal*, 60, 2, 76-84

Bailey, C., Murphy, R. and Porock, D. (2011) Professional tears: developing emotional intelligence around death and dying in emergency work. *Journal of Clinical Nursing*, 20, 23-24, 3364-3372

Bee, P., Playle, J., Lovell, K., Barnes, P., Gray, R. and Keeley, P. (2008) Service user views and expectations of UK registered mental health nurses: A systematic review of empirical research. *International Journal of Nursing Studies*, 45, 3, 442-457

Bourdreau, J., Jagosh, J and Slee, R. (2008) Patient perceptions of physicians' roles: Implications for curricula. *Academic Medicine*, 82, 8, 744-753

Boylan, O. and Loughrey, C. (2007) Developing emotional intelligence in GP trainers and registrars. *Education for Primary Care*, 18, 6, 745-748

Brackett, M., Rivers, S. and Salovey, P. (2011) Emotional intelligence: Implications for personal, social and workplace success. *Social and Personal Psychology Compass*, 5, 1, 88-103

Branfield, F. (2009) *Developing User Involvement in Social Work Education*. London: SCIE

Britton, L., and Casebourne, J. (2002) *Defining Social Inclusion*. Working Brief 136: 10-14. Centre for Economic and Social Inclusion. [Accessed 1 March 2010 at www.cesi.org.uk]

Chambers, M. and Hickey, G. (2012) *Service User Involvement in the Design and Delivery of Education and Training Programmes Leading to Registration with the Health Professions Council*. London: HCPC

Cherry, G., Fletcher, I. and O'Sullivan, H. (2014) Validating relationships among attachment, emotional intelligence and clinical communication. *Medical Education*, 48, 10, 988-997

Couldrick. L. (2008) Political Competence in Occupational Therapy. in N. Pollard, D. Sakellariou, and F. Kronenberg, (Eds.) *A Political Practice of Occupational Therapy*. London: Elsevier (pp. 21-38)

Cowden, S. and Singh, G. (2007) The 'user': Friend, foe or fetish? A critical exploration of user involvement in health and social care. *Critical Social Policy*, 27, 1, 5-23

Csikszentmihalyi, M. (1990) *Flow*. New York: Harper and Row

Department of Health (2009) *Education Commissioning for Quality*. London: The Stationery Office

Department of Health (2013) *The NHS Outcomes Framework 2014/15*. London: The Stationery Office

Empowering Learning for Social Inclusion Through Occupation (ELSiTO) *Aims*. [Accessed 3 August 2015 at http://elsito.net/?page_id=294]

Felton, A. and Stickley T. (2004) Pedagogy, power and SUI. *Journal of Psychiatric and Mental Health Nursing*, 11, 1, 89-98

Francis, R. (2013) *Report of the Mid Staffordshire NHS Foundation Trust Public Inquiry*. London: The Stationery Office

Griffiths, J., Speed, S., Horne, M. and Keeley, P. (2012) A caring professional attitude: What service users and carers seek in graduate nurses and the challenge for educators. *Nurse Education Today*, 32, 2, 121-127

Hammell, K.W. (2007) Client centred practice: Ethical obligation or professional obfuscation? *British Journal of Occupational Therapy*, 70, 6, 264-266

Harrison, D. and Sellers, A. (2008) Occupation for mental health and social inclusion. *British Journal of Occupational Therapy*, 71, 5, 215-219

Hayword, C. and Taylor, J. (2011) Eudaimonic wellbeing: Its importance and relevance to occupational therapy for humanity. *Occupational Therapy International Journal*, 18, 3, 133-141

Health and Care Professions Council (2012) *Major Change: Supplementary information for education providers*. London: HCPC

Health and Care Professions Council (2013) *Standards of Proficiency: Occupational therapists*. London: HCPC

Health and Care Professions Council (2014) *Standards of Education and Training Guidance*. London: HCPC

Higgins, A., Maguire, G., Watts, M., Creaner, M., McCann E., Rani, S. and Alexander, J. (2011) Service user involvement in mental health practitioner education in Ireland. *Journal of Psychiatric and Mental Health Nursing*, 18, 6, 519-525

Hocking, C. S. (2009) The challenge of occupation: Describing the things people do. *Journal of Occupational Science*, 16, 3, 140-150

LeBoutillier, C. and Croucher, A. (2010) Social inclusion and mental health. *British Journal of Occupational Therapy*, 73, 3, 136-139

Lequerica, A., Donnell, C. and Tate, D. (2009) Patient engagement in rehabilitation therapy: physical and occupational therapist impressions *Disability and Rehabilitation*, 31, 9, 753-760

Mayer, J.D. and Cobb, C.D. (2000) Educational policy on emotional intelligence - does it make sense? *Educational Psychology Review*, 1, 2, 163-183

Mayer, J.D. and Salovey, P. (1997) What is Emotional Intelligence? in P. Salovey and D. Sluyter (Eds) *Emotional Development and Emotional Intelligence: Implications for Educators.* New York: Basic Books

McKeown, M., Dix, J., Jones, F., Carter, B., Malihii-Shoja, L., Ernie Mallen, E. and Harrison, N. (2014) Service user involvement in practitioner education: Movement politics and transformative change. *Nurse Education Today*, 34, 8, 1175-1178

McKenna, J. (2007) Emotional intelligence training in adjustment to physical disability and illness. *International Journal of Therapy and Rehabilitation*, 14, 12, 555-556

McKenna, J. (2010) Psychosocial Support. in M. Curtin., M. Molineux. and J. Supyk Mellson. (Eds.) *Occupational Therapy and Physical Dysfunction: Enabling occupation (6th ed.).* London: Churchill Livingstone (pp. 189-210)

McKenna, J. and Mellson, J. (2013) Emotional intelligence and the occupational therapist. *British Journal of Occupational Therapy*, 76, 9, 427-430

McKenna, J. (2016) Psychosocial support, engagement and the therapeutic relationship. in M. Curtin., J.E. Adams. and M. Egan. (Eds.) *Occupational Therapy and Physical Dysfunction: Enabling Occupation, (7th ed.).* London: Elsevier (pp. 189-210)

Molineux, M. (2010) The nature of occupation. in M. Curtin, M. Molineux and J. Supyk (Eds.) *Occupational Therapy and Physical Dysfunction: Enabling occupation (6th ed.).* London: Churchill Livingstone (pp.17-26)

Morgan, A. and Jones, D. (2009) Perceptions of service user and carer involvement in healthcare education and impact on student knowledge and practice: A literature review. *Medical Teacher*, 31, 2, 82-95

Morris, D. (2001) Citizenship and community in mental health: A joint national programme for social inclusion and community partnership. *The Mental Health Review Journal*, 6, 3, 21-24.

Mullen, R., Davis, J.A. and Polatajko, H. (2011) Passion in the performing arts: Clarifying active occupational participation. *Work*, 4, 1, 15-25

Ocloo, J.E. and Fulop, N.J. (2012) Developing a 'critical' approach to patient and public involvement in patient safety in the NHS: Learning lessons from other parts of the public sector? *Health Expectations*, 15, 4, 424-432

Petrovici, A. and Dobrescu, T. (2014) The role of emotional intelligence in building interpersonal skills. *Procedia - Social and Behavioural Sciences*, 116, 1405-1410

Polatajko, H.J. (2014) A call to occupationology. *Canadian Journal of Occupational Therapy*, 8, 1, 4-7

Pollard.N., Sakellariou, D. and Kronenberg, F. (2008) *A Political Practice of Occupational Therapy.* London: Elsevier

Reed, K.D., Hocking, C.S. and Smythe, L.A. (2011) Exploring the meaning of occupation: n The case for phenomenology. *Canadian Journal of Occupational Therapy*, 78, 5, 303-310

Reid, D. (2009) Capturing presence moments: the art of mindful practice in occupational therapy. *Canadian Journal of Occupational Therapy*, 76, 3, 180-188

Repper, J. and Breeze, J. (2007) User and carer involvement in the training and education of health professionals: A review of the literature. *International Journal of Nursing Studies*, 44, 3, 511-519

ReTHINK (n.d.) [Accessed 1 March 2016 at https://www.rethink.org/best-practice-modelsandideas]

Rhodes C., Hardy, J. Padgett, K. and Symons, J. (2013) The health and well-being of service user and carer educators; a narrative enquiry into the involvement in healthcare education. *International Journal of Practice-based Learning in Health and Social Care*, 1, 1, 51-68

Rodenburg, P. (2009) *Presence: How to use positive energy for success in every situation.* London: Penguin

Rosa, S.A. and Hasselkus, B.R. (2005) Finding common ground with patients: The centrality of compatibility. *American Journal of Occupational Therapy*, 59, 2, 198-208

Royal College of Occupational Therapists (2010) *College of Occupational Therapists: Code of ethics and professional conduct.* London: RCOT

Royal College of Occupational Therapists (2014) *Learning and Development Standards for Pre-Registration Education.* London: RCOT

Schon, U-K. (2016) User and carer involvement in social work education: reasons for participation. *Scandinavian Journal of Disability Research*, 18, 2, 154-163

Senge, P., Scharmer, C.O., Jaworski, J. and Flowers, B.S. (2004) *Presence: Human purpose and the field of the future.* New York: Doubleday Broadway Publishing Group

Social Care Institute for Excellence (SCIE) (2007) Participation: Finding out what difference it makes. London: SCIE

Speers, J. (2008) Service user involvement in the assessment of a practice competency in mental health nursing. Stakeholders' views and recommendations. *Nurse Education in Practice*, 8, 2, 112-119

Straus, S.E., Tetroe, J. and Graham. I. (2009) Defining knowledge translation. *Canadian Medical Association Journal*, 181, 3-4, 165-168

Street, R.L. Jnr, Makoul, G., Arora, N.K., and Epstein, R.M. (2009) How does communication heal? Pathways linking clinician-patient communication to health outcomes. *Patient Education and Counselling*, 74, 3, 295-301

Suhaimi, A.W., Marzuki, N.A. and Mustaffa, C.S. (2014) The relationship between emotional intelligence and interpersonal communication in a disaster management context: A proposed framework. *Procedia – Social and Behavioral Sciences*, 155, 110-114

Sumsion, T. (2006) *Service User Centred Practice in Occupational Therapy: A guide to implementation.* London: Churchill Livingstone

Taylor, R.R. (2008) *The Intentional Relationship: Occupational therapy and use of self.* Philadelphia, PA: F.A. Davies

Tee, S. (2012) Service user involvement. Addressing the crisis in confidence in healthcare. *Nurse Education Today*, 32, 2, 119-120

Tickle-Degnen, L. (2014) Therapeutic rapport. in M.V. Radomski and C.A. Trombly-Latham (Eds.) *Occupational Therapy for Physical Dysfunction (7th ed.).* London: Wolters Kluwer (pp.412–427)

UK Stroke Forum [Accessed 1 March 2016 at https://www.stroke.org.uk/professionals/uk-stroke-forum 2015]

Weinberg.W (2015) Professional privilege, ethics and pedagogy. *Ethics and Social Welfare.* 9, 3, 225-239.

Weinstein, E.C. (2013) Three views of artful practice in occupational therapy. *Occupational Therapy in Mental Health*, 29, 4, 299-360

Weng, H.C., Hung, C.M., Liu, Y.T., Cheng, Y.J., Cheng-Yo, Y., Chang, C.C. and Huang, C.K. (2011) Associations between emotional intelligence and doctor burnout, job satisfaction and patient satisfaction. *Medical Education*, 45, 8, 835-42

Wilcock, A. (2006) *An Occupational Perspective of Health (2nd ed.)*. Thorofare NJ: SLACK Incorporated

Wright, N. and Stickley, T. (2013) Concepts of social inclusion, exclusion and mental health: A review of the international literature. *Journal of Psychiatric and Mental Health Nursing*, 20, 1, 71-81

Yerxa, E. J. (2011) Authentic occupational therapy. in R. Padilla and Y. Griffiths (Eds.) *A Professional Legacy: The Eleanor Clarke Slagle Lectures in occupational therapy - 1955-2010 (3rd ed.)*. Bethesda, MD: AOTA Press.

Zinker, J. (1977) *Creative Process Gestalt Therapy*. New York: Random House

Chapter 6
Youth and inclusive India

John Shanth Kumar Joseph and Hanneke van Bruggen

'One cannot have any respect or regard for men who take the position of the reformer and then refuse to see the logical consequences of that position, let alone following them out in action.' B.R. Ambedkar

Introduction

Perhaps one of the best social inclusion models could be found in the Preamble of the Constitution of India (1949) which commits,

'to secure to all its citizens: (a) Justice social, economic and political; (b) Liberty of thought, expression, belief, faith and worship; (c) Equality of status and of opportunity; and (d) promote Fraternity assuring the dignity of the individual and the unity and integrity of the Nation'.

However, this rhetoric supporting social inclusion has never been reflected in the sociopolitical, economic and cultural aspects of Indian society. On the contrary, injustice and structural exclusion has manifested in the forms of gender based violence, the practice of untouchability, ethnic disintegration, communal polarization and segregation, linguistic bias, unequal access to opportunities etc., fragmenting the very fabric of constitutionally envisioned inclusive society.

Considering the above context, India undoubtedly leans on her youth to be the agents of transformation especially when, with the median age of Indians being 29, she is set to become the youngest country in the world by 2020 (UN-Habitat 2012).

While young people aged 15–29 years in India represent approximately one-third (563 million) of the country's population (Government of India, 2013), few programs and policies exist to meet their needs. The Population Council and International Institute for Population Science (IIPS, 2010) conducted 231 interviews with key informants such as community leaders, health care providers, teachers, and youth leaders to identify the factors inhibiting and facilitating young people's safe transitions to adulthood. This youth study was the first-ever sub-national representative study of youth in India. It helped shed light on the realities of India's youth and presented recommendations for the implementation of appropriate youth-targeted programs and policies. The study covered multiple dimensions of the situation of young people, ranging from education, work and marriage to sexual and reproductive health, behaviours, attitudes, and their freedom to make informed life choices for themselves. The findings of the study have influenced youth programmes at national and local level.

The National Youth Policy (Government of India, 2014, p. 4) defined the vision of the Government of India for the youth of the country –

'to empower the youth of the country to achieve their full potential, and through them enable India to find its rightful place in the community of nations'

and identified five key areas:

Create a productive workforce;
Develop a strong and healthy generation;
Instill social values and promote community service;
Facilitate participation and civic engagement;
Support youth at risk and create equitable opportunity for all.

Although there were already a number of youth, groups, movements, organisations and institutions trying to act as a support base in the process of youth building for the future, these efforts were insufficient given the size of the youth population. In line with the Youth Policy and as a reaction to the challenges young people face in India, a youth platform called Youth Empowered in Action for Humanity (YEAH) was developed in 2012 and officially established in May 2014. YEAH is committed to empower young people for youth led actions which should lead to social transformation. They organise different initiatives, like workshops, demonstrations, camps and aim for a broad social movement of the youth to create an inclusive society.

Hereafter the challenges for young people in India and the reasons for establishing YEAH will be described and focused on the methodology used and the concrete initiatives undertaken so far.

Challenges to young people in India

The young people in the age group of 10-24 years constitute one of the precious resources of India, characterized by their growth and development and a phase of vulnerability often influenced by several intrinsic and extrinsic factors that affect their health and safety. Nearly 10-30 per cent of young people suffer from health impacting behaviours and conditions that need the urgent attention of policy makers and public health professionals (Singh & Gopalkrishna, 2014). Nutritional disorders (both malnutrition and over-nutrition), tobacco use, harmful alcohol use, other substance use, high risk sexual behaviours, stress, common mental disorders, and injuries (road traffic injuries, suicides, violence of different types), specifically affect this population and may have long lasting impact over their life trajectories. Healthy life-style and health promotion policies and programmes are central to the health of youth, driven by robust population-based studies (Singh & Gopalkrishna, 2014).

The first, and the foremost concern of today's youth in India is better education, employment driven training and a brighter future. Youth also want skill based education and job placement to be a part of every higher institution. More emphasis should be placed on career oriented courses which go beyond text book learning to connect with real life scenarios (TUNING India, 2014).

Although the youth unemployment rate in India decreased to 12.90% in 2013 from 18.10% in 2012 by 2050, millions of youth in India are going to be unemployed. With a million jobs required every month—eight million are required every year until 2050—dominant castes across various regions are reacting violently to unfulfilled aspirations (Abhishek, 2016).

Today's youth is also very concerned with the issue of corruption in Indian society, as was evident when most of the protestors in 2011 in the campaign led by Anna Hazare (a 72 year old ex-army man) against corruption were young people (Kaur, 2013). A series of demonstrations and protests across India brought together youth to engage in political action with a special focus on rampant corruption, deteriorating economic fabric, policy loopholes and global recessions. The movement gained momentum from 5 April 2011, when anti-corruption activist Anna Hazare began a hunger strike at the Jantar Mantar (the Sundial Monument) in New Delhi. In 2012 the movement was reinvigorated and some of the founders became politicians. However the struggle to address corruption at all levels became a political drama and the movement collapsed (a film biography was made about the life of Hazare, released in late 2016, although reviews have been highly critical of its simplified portrayal).

The foundation of YEAH

This anti-corruption initiative misled the youth of India to believe in the constructed conscience as the truth and *the* only solution for transformation. The youth hardly questioned the rationale, political intricacy, relevance, process and actions of the movement, and though a few alternative perspectives were shared, the mainstream watered them down. Recognition of this problem was one of the motives to start YEAH and focus on pragmatic solutions rather than on preventing wrongs in society.

The three founders of YEAH, Sonia Dominica, Elango Stanislaus and John Shant Kumar Joseph, know each other from college days when all three studied social work. Elango is from TamilNadu in the South-East, while Sonia and John are from Karnataka in South-West India, but all were part of the same rights-based university student movement. After their studies they have continued to work with students and youth in India. John also works with student movements across Asia and Pacific. John is the executive director of YEAH and his passion is community mobilisation, training and advocacy. A fourth member has been added to the YEAH team, Ajesh (coordinator), who is one of the students who was part of YEAH's training. After his bachelor degree in commerce and law he joined as a volunteer.

Hanneke van Bruggen met John Shant in the first World Conference on Community Based Rehabilitation (CBR) in Agra, India in 2011. She visited John in Bangalore and stayed in contact with the developments of Yeah. In 2013 Hanneke was sent as a Tuning expert for a feasibility study in higher education in two states of India and learned more about the youth/ students of India.

The founders of YEAH found that in their experience and analysis youth work in India was mostly isolated rather than linked with reality. Two major issues play a significant role in youth work:

Lack of perspective hinders the development of a people-centric perspective, isolates youth from being part of the wider society, and creates a pseudo identity, society, values and culture and manipulates his or her youth-hood and energy.

Lack of perspective leads to a lack of vision. Further, the lack of vision confirms inequality, discrimination and violence as socially acceptable phenomenon at all levels especially among youth.

YEAH is primarily founded as a platform for youth empowerment and youth led action. Though it has been registered under the Trust Act in 2014, it has been working since 2012 mainly as a capacity building initiative for the youth of Karnataka. Its vision is to educate, engage, equip and empower youth for a transformational society.

The mission of YEAH is to:

- Educate youth through continued introspection of their socio-economic, political and cultural relationships, practices and living;
- Engage youth in communities to witness the relatedness of their realities and issues of marginalisation;
- Equip youth to address oppression and suffering of the self and that of the communities;
- Empower youth to re-engage as agents of transformation of communities free from marginalisation through youth-led initiatives

YEAH has chosen their interventions to be two-dimensional: (1) Responding to the need of transformation of the internal oppression that youth face in their day-to-day living and (2) channeling their internal transformation to influence the transformation of the larger society.

Applied methodology/philosophy

The ideas and methods YEAH is applying are derived from a mix of philosophers, of which two are particular important.

Dr. B.R. Ambedkar

The visionary philosopher Dr. B.R. Ambedkar was the chief architect of the Indian Constitution who led a number of social movements to secure human rights for the oppressed and depressed sections of Indian society. He gained international recognition as a liberator of humanity from social and economic injustice. Ambedkar (1979, p. VIII) says:

'If you ask me, my ideal would be a society based on liberty, equality and fraternity....
an ideal society should be mobile, should be full of channels for conveying a change
taking place in one part to other parts.'

Ambedkar fully endorsed Dewey's emphasis on education as a means to change the world and not merely to understand it. Dewey held that democracy cannot go forward unless the intelligence of the mass of people is educated to understand the social realities of their own time (Dewey, 1916). Ambedkar's important contribution to the education sector was his belief that education is something which ought to be brought within the reach of every one. His efforts for the uplift of the underprivileged so that all people in society get equal opportunities have inspired YEAH to work with the deprived youth to achieve justice and equal rights in society.

Paolo Freire

Freire and Ambedkar were towering figures among radical social theorists of the last century (Simon, 2015). The primary concern for Ambedkar is the liberation of the Dalits (untouchables), the people of the lower strata of Indian society. The situation of Dalits was much like the poor of the Northeast of Brazil. Therefore Freire's pedagogy of education, creating spaces where concepts of justice and hope emerge and are sustained, is of great interest to YEAH's leadership. These ideas find a fertile ground largely because of their consistency with the thought of the historic Dalit leader, B.R. Ambedkar.

What YEAH finds particular attractive in Freire's approach is the experiential learning theory that offers a dynamic theory based on a learning cycle driven by the resolution of the dual dialectics of action/reflection and experience/abstraction. These two dimensions define a holistic learning space wherein learning transactions take place between individuals and the environment. The process of learning from experience is ubiquitous, present in human activity everywhere all the time. Freire believed that through such active participation, people come to recognize their need for more knowledge or training, and that this motivation is key to successful learning. Additionally, though, Freire emphasized dialogue as the only legitimate pedagogical method, claiming that teacher and students must be seen as equal. According to Freire (1967), freedom will be the result of praxis—informed action—when a balance between theory and practice is achieved. Freire (1970) claimed that by learning skills relevant to their harsh lives, people can be empowered to create a better society. Education should encourage reflection on the values and ideals people share, and should motivate people to engage in community service. Freire warned that the traditional style of education only promotes the status quo by teaching the things people in power want others to learn.

Initiatives of YEAH

Over the period of three years YEAH has reached about 24,000 students on an average per year between the ages of 9 to 23 year old with training, events, seminars and through the media on issues such as caste, communalism, gender, child sexual abuse, education, regionalism, racism, labour rights, sustainable development, human rights, leadership, volunteering, life skills and etc. in 25 schools and colleges in urban and rural Bangalore as well as Mangalore, Mysore, Hassan and Harihar.

The YEAH initiatives have been born out of the need to engage the youth in transforming themselves as change agents and are structured in the following 10 core initiatives with each their specific aims:

1. Young Documenters Forum
2. Peace NeT
3. GenNet
4. Inter-Act
5. Young Educators Forum
6. Youth for Sustainable Living
7. Young Workers Forum

8. Youth for inter-caste Dialogue
9. Young Professionals Network
10. Inter-Lingual Youth Forum

Hereafter the background and the aims of 5 of the 10 initiatives will be given in order to demonstrate the ideas of YEAH.

1. Young Documenters Forum

'Until lions have their own historians, tales of the hunt shall always glorify the hunter.' This statement by the African writer Chinua Achebe has always been proved true in the context and practice of mainstreaming struggles of the communities for rights and dignity around the globe. It applies even more so in India where the individuals and institutions structurally fabricate the history of communities (as perhaps is exemplified in the Hazare film described above) to benefit their own agenda and are celebrated as heroes, continue to play saviours and are questioned too little. Hence, it becomes our duty to establish the subaltern history, i.e. a post-colonial history from the perspective of the lower classes in Indian society. Therefore, YEAH has created this forum of youth to:

- Document the struggles of the individuals and communities;
- Inspire and support youth to consciously be involved in mainstreaming and recounting struggles of the society and to become a platform for young writers, artists, cartoonists, poets, and audio visual practitioners etc.,
- To come together for building a pro-community perspective

2. Peace Net

The very idea of India as pluralist society is explained by the co-option and co-existence of people from diverse culture, religion and language, with unique personal and community experience. Indian values and ethos are deep rooted in multi religious and multi-cultural identities of communities of India. Every religion is unique in itself with each of them having its own followers cutting across all identities. But in recent times, religious diversity has been used to create hatred towards each other; in 2013 a document released by the Home Ministry said there were 479 incidents of communal violence that year, apart from 107 people killed, 1,647 people including 794 Hindus, 703 Muslims and 200 policemen were injured. These figures are double those of 2012 (Bharti, 2013).

As YEAH's voice against communalism (communalism is a term used in South Asia to represent ideologies centred on particular communities, especially religious communities), a forum is created to help youth to:

- Understand and recognise faith (religious and non-religious) identities;
- Explore concepts of peace and harmony in one's own faith and practices;
- Converge thoughts and practices to celebrate unity in diversities;
- Combat communalism

3. GenNet

The level of violence and discrimination against women and Lesbian Gay Bisexual Transgender and Queer (LGBTQ) has increased significantly. This trend is supported by section 377 of the Indian Penal Code which makes sex with persons of the same gender punishable. Between the years of 2001 and 2011, the number of crimes against women rose an alarming 59%, the number one crime being rape (*Government of India*, 2012). This social structure paves the way for discrimination against these communities which results in violation of their basic rights as humans. The women and the LGBTQ community are portrayed as bearing the blame for the violence and discrimination toward them, and the official solution is to control their actions.

The effect of this policy of control has been to widen the gap between the genders, leading to further marginalisation. Dialogue is one of the solutions to eliminate the gender gap and bring gender equity. Genet is an open platform for youth from different sexual orientations to gather and

- Understand and respect different sexual identities.
- To create platforms to dialogue on gender realities.
- Build new partnership across sexual identities to address discriminations.

4. Young Educators Forum

The primary role of education is to facilitate the process of learning or acquisition of knowledge, skills and values. This depends on the one who facilitates, the educators, but today they are caught between their roles and their challenges.
The challenges faced by educators today are many, such as:

- Changing education scenario: how far does the content to be made relevant for the market, which learning methodologies are needed?
- Changing student realities: is the aim of education for employability or learning to learn?, dichotomy between the values and application, between student reality versus student dream.
- Changing institution: Business versus mission, withdrawal of state support, survivability of institution, scarcity of resources, non-conducive learning environment.
- Changing society: educating towards human development, equality and justice in a society of growing disparities, no accountability, profit-centered values.

In spite of knowing this, a lot of youth take up the mission of education with a dream of transformation. As a youth movement dedicated to transformation YEAH recognises the important role that the educators play. Towards the effort of concretising our support, YEAH wishes to partner the process of transformation with young educators through Young Educators Forum with the following objectives:

- Create network and support groups of young educators to address day-to-day issues and challenges;
- Understand the concept of education as a tool for transformation
- Create and identify best practices in education for transformation

5. Youth for Sustainable Living:

At one time there were no soft drink alternatives to water, but now water has become an alternative to soft drinks which are especially preferred among youth. The rapid increase in soft drink sales and their acceptance shows the control of the market, operated by international corporations such as Pepsi-Cola and Coca-Cola, over young people, which is evidence of increasing disposable income and lifestyle quality. This has been portrayed as part of the process of development for India in its transition to becoming a developed country through encouraging foreign investment, but has involved lobbying and pressure on governments by multinational companies (Williams, 2015). The consequences of this process of development and effects of it on the resources are few of the questions which are still unanswered or have been ignored at large.

'We are witnessing what can be described as market fundamentalism. People believe in the market as if it was a god. There seems to be a sense that nothing could ever happen without it. A free world market for everything has to be established – a world market that functions according to the interests of the corporations and capitalist money... One thing remains generally overlooked: The abstract wealth created for accumulation implies the destruction of nature as concrete wealth' (Werlhof, 2015, p. 4).

To assist the youth to come out of the consumerist culture and help restore a more sustainable living cycle, this forum calls to:

- Critically examine practices of development
- Understand sustainable development, dimensions and viability
- Create and or promote models for sustainable development
- Place sustainable living as a resistance movement against market driven living.

This structure helps to mobilise youth, although YEAH struggles to organise workshops and regular initiatives due to lack of funds. However they managed to organise smaller events such as a midnight march and marathon to voice against violence on women, workshops and candle light vigils for peace, ten-day workshops on different human rights issues.

A 10 days Human Rights Education workshops was organised with the name 'Left Rights' to mark the International Human Rights day as well as an effort to bring discussions on rights among the youth. The topics for the ten days were: concept of human rights and its application, right to freedom, violence against women, sexuality and human rights, reservation, right to freedom of religion, child rights, self-determination, privatisation & human rights and human rights based development. 3800 students from 8 institutions took part in these workshops.

Trainings & Workshops

1. Campus Based: To complement and solidify the academic learning of students, YEAH conducts three levels of interventions:

(a) Foundation course 'Socio-Political Analysis': This course attempts to familiarise undergraduate students with the main political, economic and social developments that have taken place in India since independence in specific relation to the marginalised population and also equip the students to address their day-to-day issues vis-à-vis that of the marginalised population as the future leaders. About 2400 students have passed through the course.

b) Academic outreach 'Converging Campus & Community': An initiative to assist students to witness different social realities around their campuses, introspect and find connections with their own realities and contribute ideas, skills and solutions. 700 students have taken part in these outreach programs.

(c) Rural Exposure Camp: Rural exposure camps are part of YEAH's effort in bridging urban and rural disconnect. These camps assist students to experience rural life, study and understand rural contexts and challenges and reflect on the role of the student and youth in empowering communities. The camps have been organised on specific issues affecting rural communities such as mining, farmer's suicides and sustainable development.

2. Issue Based: Issue based workshops and training programs are another form of YEAH's engagement with youth. Series of trainings and workshops are organised in Bangalore, Mangalore and Mysore addressing the issues of gender, child sexual abuse, social leadership, sexuality and development. 9500 Students, 100 educators and 1000 parents have participated in these workshops

3. Partnered: In collaboration with different change agencies and institutions, a total 18,000 students together with 400 activists we reached through trainings on Rights, Gender, Trafficking, Legal Aid, Conflict, Media, Caste, Sustainable Development and Life Skills.

YEAH Academy

Besides the activities under the 10 core initiatives YEAH has established the YEAH Academy committed to strategically empower people for action. It focuses on personality development and the social aspect of individuals. They offer training, workshops, exposures and learning modules to address the empowerment issues of individuals, with any qualification and in different sectors, institutions, organisations, groups and communities. These are customised programs for different age groups (7-14 yrs, 15-20 yrs, and 20+) and are the main source of funding for all YEAH's work.

Sammanasu Memorial Centre

Lately YEAH has as well established the Sammanasu Memorial Centre (SMC) a space for experimental learning. A centre for agro-based research and education, a drop-in centre for the rural youth, a centre for urban-rural youth exchange and possibly a retreat and rejuvenation centre.

With all these initiatives and interventions, YEAH hopes the youth of India to become the torch bearers of an inclusive society.

Conclusion

The current international, national and local situations pose a great challenge to the youth. These challenges push the youth into a culture of silence, where everything looks fine for them and makes them loose the power of critical thinking. Critical thinking liberates the individuals and when they lose it, the very essence of their life is lost. Neo-globalisation buys young minds and indoctrinates them with self-centric and destructive ideology. 'I' occupies the significant part of their language by eliminating the language of 'we' 'us' and 'others'.

These challenges alter the lives of the youth and make them search for (new) alternatives. These challenges are based on contrasts between urban-rural, rich-poor, men-women, popular political ideology, environmental alterations, development paradigms and other notions. Certain alternatives worked in the past and new alternatives emerge based on different challenges.

YEAH aims at bridging the gap between challenges and alternatives. YEAH does not aim at providing tailor-made solutions to the existing and emerging challenges, instead it becomes the launch pad where the youth find their alternatives.

There are youth who challenge the existing popular paradigms, a dissent to oppressive ideology, redefining genders, challenging the ideologies of caste, class and race. The situation is not bleak and the way forward will be to do research and development, document untold stories, capacity building, interaction and activities with communities, workshops, advocacy, development of a website and face-book pages and movement and network building in all the core areas of YEAH.

'It is not in the stars to hold our destiny but in ourselves' William Shakespeare.

References

Ambedkar, B.R. (1979) *Dr. Babasaheb Ambedkar: Writings and Speeches, Vol.1* (compiled by Vasant Moon), Education Department, Government of Maharashtra, Bombay [Accessed 15th March 2021 at: https://www.mea.gov.in/Images/attach/amb/Volume_01.pdf]

Ambedkar, B.R. (1982) *Dr. Babasaheb Ambedkar: Writings and Speeches, Vol.2* (compiled by Vasant Moon), Education Department, Government of Maharashtra, Bombay [Accessed 15th March 2021 at: https://www.mea.gov.in/Images/attach/amb/Volume_02.pdf]

Abhishek W (2016) By 2050, millions of youth in India are going to be unemployed: Report reveals how, [Accessed 15th March 2021 at: https://www.youthkiawaaz.com/2016/05/lack-of-jobs-and-unemployment-in-india/

Bharti, J. (2013) Government releases data of riot victims identifying religion, *The Times of India*, 24 September 2013 [Accessed 15th March 2021 at: https://timesofindia.indiatimes.com/india/government-releases-data-of-riot-victims-identifying-religion/articleshow/22998550.cms]

Constitution of India, Pre-Amble (1949), [Accessed 15th March 2021 at: http://www.legalserviceindia.com/legal/article-750-preamble-to-the-indian-constitution.html#:~:text=Preamble%20declares%20India%20to%20be,socialist%2C%20secular%20and%20democratic%20republic.&text=The%20objectives%20stated%20by%20the,and%20

integrity%20of%20the%20nation.]

Dewey, J, (1916/1997) *Democracy and Education: An Introduction to the Philosophy of Education*, New York: Simon and Schuster

Freire, P. (1967) *Education, the Practice of Freedom*. London: Writers and Readers Publishing Cooperative

Freire, P. (1970) Pedagogy of the Oppressed. London: Continuum

Government of India (2012) *Crime in India*, [Accessed 15th March 2021 at: https://ncrb.gov.in/en/table-crime-india-2012-2]

Government of India (2013) *The twelfth five year plan vol.II.* Government of India, Planning Commission [Accessed 15th March 2021 at: https://mofpi.nic.in/sites/default/files/vol_2.pdf.pdf]

Government of India (2014) *National Youth Policy*, Ministry of Youth Affairs and Sports [Accessed 29 November 2016 at http://www.youthpolicy.org/national/India_2014_National_Youth_Policy.pdf]

International Institute for Population Sciences (IIPS), (2010) *The Youth in India: Situation and Needs 2006-2007*, Mumbai: IIPS, [Accessed 29 November 2016 at https://www.macfound.org/media/article_pdfs/2010PGY_YouthInIndiaReport.pdf]

Ramandeep, K. (2013) *Problems faced by youth in India, Maps of India*, [Accessed 29 November 2016 at www.mapsofindia.com/my-india/india/problems-faced-by-youth-in-india]

Simon, L. R. (2015) *Paulo Freire and B.R. Ambedkar: In Comparative Perspective.* International Symposium on Annihilation of Caste: The Unfinished Legacy of Dr B.R. Ambedkar, Waltham MA: The Center for Global Development and Sustainability, The Heller School at Brandeis University

Singh, S. and Gopalkrishna, G. (2014) Health behaviours and problems among young people in India: Cause for concern & call for action, *Indian Journal of Medical Research*, 140, 2, 185–208

TUNING India (2014) *Feasibility study final report,* TUNING Academy [Accessed 15th March 2021 at: http://tuningacademy.org/wp-content/uploads/2015/01/Tuning_India_Feasibility_Study_Final_Report.pdf]

UN-Habitat (2012) *State of the Urban Youth 2012/2013*, United Nations Human Settlements Programme, Nairobi, Kenya [Accessed 15th March 2021 at: https://unhabitat.org/the-state-of-urban-youth-20122013-youth-in-the-prosperity-of-cities]

Werlhof, von C. (2017) *Globalization and Neoliberal Policies. Are there Alternatives to Plundering the Earth, Making War and Destroying the Planet?* [Accessed 15th March 2021 at https://www.globalresearch.ca/the-consequences-of-globalization-and-neoliberal-policies-what-are-the-alternatives/7973]

Williams, S.N. (2015) The incursion of 'Big Food' in middle-income countries: a qualitative documentary case study analysis of the soft drinks industry in China and India. *Critical Public Health*, 25, 4, 455-473.

Section 5
Projects

This section introduces diverse projects from different continents and in different phases of development. They range from a personal development projects around meaningful occupation to large multisectoral projects involving private, public and third sectors. This section demonstrates how universities can develop socially accountable projects which involve new learning situations for students, and presents an example of a project proposal as well as a successfully completed community based rehabilitation project in which health, education and the public sector work together.

The first chapter from Hayama gives a wonderful narrative of how the author, following a stroke and recognising the benefits he obtained through occupational therapy, developed a day service centre in Japan through which other people could experience meaningful occupation.

Simo's Renaissance community project focuses on children's wellbeing and social inclusion in the context of high unemployment, job insecurity and poverty in Catalonia in Spain. The project has two angles: tacking the causes of poverty through encouraging social entrepreneurship, and addressing the consequences of poverty, such as emotional and nutritional problems through cultural activities and health promotion. At the same time, this work provides students at the University of Vic with service learning placements and research opportunities.

The following chapter by Minato, again from Japan, reveals the importance of university leadership in his local community. His project concerns employment opportunities for people with mental health problems. Minato describes how traditional approaches supported by state provision and cultural stereotypes around mental illness have made it difficult for people to move beyond sheltered workshops into inclusive and regular employment. He reports the successes of a flexible scheme in which people can organise their own working patterns.

Mulzheim and Hemmeler-Händel, present the early stages of a project proposal for homeless people in Vienna, Austria, using the participatory quality development approach. Their discussion covers the complexities and the necessity of building partnerships with residents, community members, administrators and other professionals.

In the following chapter from the Philippines David sets out a well established CBR programme: Project therapy, Education and Assimilation of Children with Handicap (TEACH). Established in collaboration with municipal authorities, the programme provides services for children from impoverished families and provides a range of activities, from therapy to education and vocational training, while also working to promote inclusive attitudes towards children with disabilities. The project actively involves parents in the support of therapy session and the upkeep of the premises.

The final chapter by Morishima and Diago is again from Japan, and describes innovative actions with the community to promote skill development, care and support between neighbours and across generations. This extension of occupational practice beyond the treatment of specific illnesses and conditions to developing community support networks addresses the authors belief that all people will at some time benefit from these ties when they encounter difficulty.

Chapter 7
Looking at occupations
as a stroke survivor

Yasuaki Hayama

I have lived in Japan since I was born in 1965. I am a sixty year-old man. I have become a person with right hemiplegia because I suffered from a left cerebral hemorrhage. Then I started my second life. My second life has been more meaningful and dramatic since I encountered occupational therapy, which is wonderful and revived my life. Encountering the concept of occupation, which is practical and important, colours, supports and empowers my second life. I will write the story.

Travel as an occupation

I was born the second son of a part-time farmer in Fukuoka, Japan. I liked to play baseball in elementary school, do kendo (Japanese fencing) in middle school, and play a guitar and ride a motorcycle in high school. I was interested in cars and girls rather than studies in university. It was typical in Japan at that age.

I had worked as an office clerk or sales representative in a company. I questioned my ordinary life and I longed for faraway lands. Perhaps the reason I wanted to go to another continent was that my grandparents migrated to Peru and my father was born in Peru.

I left for Peru from Japan as a backpacker. I walked around the continent through Peru, Patagonia, and Argentina. I sailed from Brazil to Italy and went to the east of the Eurasian continent. I arrived in Japan after 10 months. It was an irreplaceable experience.

After I came back to Japan, I got married, had three children, and bought a house. I had absorbed the occupation of teaching students, education, as a teacher of accountancy in my thirties and forties. I was busy working, a workaholic, in fact. I realized that my occupational balance had collapsed when the disease hit me.

Hardships from my left cerebral hemorrhage and occupational therapy

In winter 2006, when I was 40 years old, I collapsed in a meeting room at the school I worked for. I had suffered a left cerebral hemorrhage. I was admitted to a hospital in Fukuoka, then began rehabilitation immediately.

I had right hemiplegia from a left cerebral hemorrhage. I had proprioceptive sense disorder and motor dysfunction. I was in a wheelchair (see photo 1 overleaf).

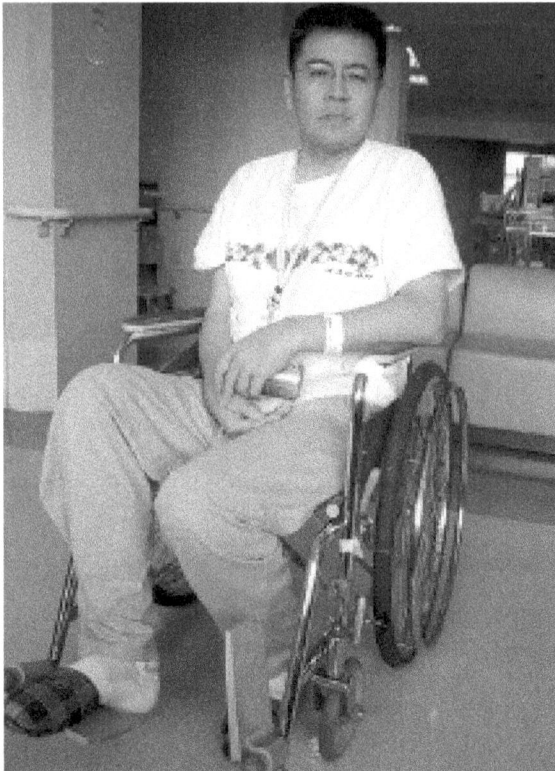

Photo 1. Me in a wheelchair

There were: a physical therapist who trained me to walk between parallel bars, a speech therapist who trained me to speak, and an occupational therapist who trained me on daily actions, or occupations. Daily actions, occupations, included cooking. I was surprised because my image of rehabilitation was hardship and pain. But cooking is one kind of rehabilitation…

In an occupational therapy room in a hospital:

Me: Every day is humdrum. Can we do something interesting?
OT: I agree. As long as we can do it in the hospital.
Me: Anything is OK?
OT: Yes.
Me: Well, let's cook and eat Japanese-style pasta. I'm good at cooking it. I used to cook it when I was traveling, and I made it for my kids at my house.
OT: Good. First let's make a plan!

My right hand was paralyzed. So my occupational therapist and I wrote a plan with my left hand, selected materials, prepared, cooked, served—success!

I ate Japanese pasta that I cooked using my left hand for the first time in my life with my therapists. Of course, it was especially great!

Curry and rice and grilled steaks cooked outside while camping are delicious because of the environment and process. I cooked Japanese tasting pasta using only my left hand with the assistance of my occupational therapist. The taste became many times better through the process and human environment and my sense of accomplishment. The joy of accomplishing the occupation with only my left hand led to the joy in living and started raising my self-confidence. Moreover, I started to look to the future a little; 'I will do this next time' or 'Maybe I'll do that tomorrow!' The occupation of cooking pasta started reconstructing my body and mind.

Photo 2: My occupational therapist, my speech therapist, and me eating Japanese pasta two weeks after onset, 2006>

Discharge from hospital and use of a day service center

After discharge from the hospital, I went to a day service center and received physical rehabilitation services. However physical recovery stopped after six months from onset, the same as on the recovery curve of stroke patients that I found on the internet. It was cruel. I wondered what the meaning of physical training was for an incurable body. I couldn't afford to spend my energy on making a miracle whose possibility is less than 1%. I had to return to work, earn, and take care of my family, recovery or no recovery.

In the hospital I had rehabilitation for recovery from paralysis. Leaving the hospital, I had rehabilitation without recovery. I saw there is a deep irrationality in the Japanese health care system. But there is no irrationality in occupation-focused occupational therapy (Canadian Association of Occupational Therapists, 1997). Occupational therapy gave me the environment for enabling self-care, enjoyment, and productive activities, enabling occupation, and it covered psychological aspects without the heroic machines used in physical therapy in a hospital. Moreover, my meaningful occupation, cooking Japanese pasta, was enabled. The sense and knowledge of the experience remained after discharge from the hospital as my embodied knowledge. It was amazing and made a strong connection to my second life.

There was no occupational therapist in the day service center, so I did my own style occupational therapy. I did driving, tea ceremony, pottery, going to movies, taking a trip, visiting historical places, cooking, drinking beer cheerfully, eating Japanese cuisine with my left hand, going to a museum, fighting with my left hand, and listening to the music of Led Zeppelin and the Beatles again. My life became independent, step by step through many occupations. It's not only my daily life but also my entire life.

Establishing Keyaki-Dori Day Service Center

I resigned from my company as a result of an unsuccessful discussion about returning to the job, 14 months after onset. I established Care Planets Corporation and started to run the Keyaki-Dori Day Service Center at the age of forty-two. I took the name from a favorite company, Lonely Planet, which published the travel guides I had used (with a dictionary) during my trips.

Why did I establish a company and open a day service center? The first reason was to make a living for my family and myself. The next reason was the lack of occupational therapy in the town where I lived. I also wanted to prove that a person with disabilities can work and the experiences of disabilities can contribute to modifying environments for care and rehabilitation.

Programmes offering meaningful occupations for older people became a selling point of my day service center. That's how I began my occupation, business, as representative director.

Photo 3: Keyaki-Dori Day Service Center, 2008

Encounter with occupational science

I encountered occupational science and occupation via Professor Hiromi Yoshikawa in the Prefectural University of Hiroshima six months after establishing Keyaki-Dori Day Service Center at the age of forty-three in 2008 (Yoshikawa, 2008). That is when I learned the foundations of occupational science that allow me to describe my occupational understanding in this chapter.

Human beings are not only about physical function. After I came to know occupations as a flow experience (Csikszentmihalyi, 1990), I was filled with exultant feelings. I'm a person doing occupations, not *a disabled person*. I don't have to think about right hemiplegia at all.

I received a lot of smiles and felt joy when I supported the meaningful occupations of older persons or persons with disabilities in a day service center.

Entering a graduate school

I opened a second day service center and published a book, That's Why I Like Occupational Therapy, at the age 47 in 2012 (Hayama, 2012). I was able to publish an English version of the book, Look at What You Can Do! with the enormous help of Timothy Buthod who is an English teacher in the Prefectural University of Hiroshima and Prof. Yoshikawa (Hayama, 2014). I have continued to give lectures talking about occupation, occupational therapy, and the Keyaki-Dori Day Service Center for occupational therapy students in universities and practitioners, including therapists in workshops sponsored by professional organizations. Nine years have passed since I broke down. I have given more than 100 lectures in seven years. I have talked occupation to 14,000 people. My meaningful occupation, management, then changed to education. I can do occupations such as administration and education although my paralysis has remained. That is enough to feel happiness.

But the challenge and joy from now on is teaching my children. It involves doing it, feeling it and making it. When I think about this, I was very regretful that I could not play catch with my son. When I was an elementary student, I played catch with my father until it got dark. He taught me baseball. I remember I imagined playing catch and was exulted when having our first son after two daughters. But my reality is 'right hemiplegia'.

I thought about my occupations. Playing catch means to pass on important things from father to son along with baseball. If so, I think that I have to seek another form of occupation. I have gone to the movies and traveled by train, bus, and taxi around Tokyo with my son. But it is different from the way I played catch with my father. The differences are not expenses and money but how much effort the father makes. Although I can't find good words, the occupation of going to the movies and visiting Tokyo by train and playing catch are different in their meaning, view of life, and educational value. I spent some time reflecting on my position and what I could do. My strengths are that I spend a lot of time sitting and I have the uncommon experience of disability. My weakness is that I cannot move fast and use my body easily. What can I do using my left hand while sitting? I decided I would go to graduate school, research the welfare of persons with disabilities, and write a thesis. They would demonstrate my values as a father to my children. In 2013, I entered the Graduate School of Human Science of Seinan Gakuin University in Fukuoka.

The entrance exam, which included an essay and an interview, was modified, allowing the use of a computer and longer writing time and a longer interview because I have mild aphasia and cognitive dysfunction. I was able to pass because of these accommodations.

I went to classes at night driving my modified car, took notes left-handed, and worked on assignments using a computer. I can do these things even though I have paralysis. The possibilities of my life were tremendously expanded through these occupations. My research theme was 'Ethnography of classes in cooking with one hand: A life construction process in Yume-no-Mizuumi Mura' (that means Lake of Dreams in Japanese).

It was qualitative research and made the most of my experience of disability. People with more experience of hemiplegia teach cooking to people with less experience of hemiplegia every day in the Yume-no-Mizuumi Mura, a facility under the Care Insurance Law (Usuda & Fujiwara, 2003). I analyzed and discussed how persons who first had disabilities in middle age, reconstruct their own lives in respect of cooking, teaching cooking, learning cooking, environmental factors, and personal factors.

There will be more possibilities to do research and collaborate with occupational therapists because I am a person who has experience of living with disabilities for nine years.

I finished graduate school after two tough years in spring 2015. What can I bring to my son? The answer whether my children received something will only be clear after I'm gone. But I can believe my children get something now. Something like a confidence built in mine.

Photo 4: Receiving a master's degree at the graduation ceremony, 2015

Necessity of self-confidence through occupation in rehabilitation

Rather than accomplishment, I felt relief and despondency when my advisor called to say my master's thesis had passed. I was relieved because I didn't have to correct my paper any more. But I had gradually recognized changes in myself, as I flew to a place where I had a lecture, participated in a meeting, talked, and was regarded with admiration. Self-confidence was building like a tower. Although I had taught accountancy to university students and given lectures on corporate taxes, I have survived with difficulty after the cerebral hemorrhage. I don't have the brain function for teaching accountancy and corporate taxes any more. So I have lost confidence for nine years. I have focused relentlessly on survival. I had ceased to exist as a teacher of accountancy and corporate taxes. But now I got a master's degree through two years of occupations such as study, research surveys, and writing a thesis. I got the master's degree which is evidence of a competent person in society, and I have confidence.

It's the first time in nine years. Maybe I searched theories, sometimes offered a counterargument, persuaded others, or overemphasized to protect myself for nine years because of lack of confidence. I might have fooled others because I could not afford to be honest. In other words, many persons who have disabilities in midlife may lose confidence as well as physical function and struggle with friction, conflict, distress, removal from society, isolation, nothingness, emptiness, and even death.

This confidence is different from the confidence from a sense of accomplishment and self-efficacy when I cook pasta. This confidence is from acquiring outcomes through occupations that need more effort and longer periods of time. This experience is a fact. The fact is true. These occupations can be added to my life.

Acknowledgement

The author would like to acknowledge with thanks the contribution of Hiromi Yoshikawa for her contribution to the editing and translation of this chapter.

References

Canadian Association of Occupational Therapists (1997) *Enabling Occupation: An occupational therapy perspective.* Ottawa: CAOT. (Japanese translation by Yoshikawa, H. et al, 2000, Daigaku Kyoiku Syuppan)

Csikszentmihalyi, M. (1990) *Flow: The psychology of optimal experience.* New York: Harper & Row. (Japanese translation by Imamura, H., 1996. Sekai Shisosya)

Hayama, Y. (2012) *That's Why I Like Occupational Therapy,* Tokyo: Miwa-Shoten (in Japanese)

Hayama, Y. (2014) *Look at What You Can Do!* Tokyo: Miwa-Shoten

Yoshikawa, H. (2008) *What is Occupation? An introduction to occupational science.* Tokyo: Ishiyaku-Shuppan (in Japanese)

Usuda, K. and Fujiwara, S. (2003) *The Life of Hemiplegia Who can Do Anything: Some wisdoms change your life,* Tokyo: Seikai-Sya (in Japanese)

Chapter 8
Renaissance project: Occupational based intervention to promote wellbeing and social inclusion

Salvador Simó Algado

Introduction

Occupation based projects can promote wellbeing and social inclusion. In order to enhance its social relevance and to have a real impact, occupational therapy must take better account of the political (Pollard et al, 2008), economic and ecological (Simó Algado & Townsend, 2015) dimensions of the context of practice.

As a profession we have to flow in a society defined as liquid by Bauman (2005a) characterised by constant change. The real power in society is moving from the national states to the big economic corporations (Castells, 2005). The traditional paths to social inclusion, such as having a good education, are no longer a guarantee. Although individuals cannot control their context they are blamed for their failure in this competitive capitalist system (Bauman, 2005b).

The current context in Spain is marked by the proliferation of poverty (28.1%), unemployment (25%) and job insecurity (EAPN, 2014). The deconstruction of the welfare state translates into health, social, and educational cuts by Government. These cuts affect the social cohesion, wellbeing and welfare of the population, jeopardizing its future development (Navarro, 2006).

This chapter narrates the development of the *Renaissance* community project. The core of the project is meaningful occupation. It focuses on improving children's wellbeing, social inclusion and educational occupational performance. It develops a community-based intervention empowering the children, the parents and the teachers. The project is led by the third Sector (University of Vic - Universitat Central de Catalunya UVic-UCC and Sinia School), in partnership with the public (Vic City council, Osona Mental Health) and private sector (La Caixa Bank Foundation).

As poverty is a key problem in the community and affects children's wellbeing (CSDH, 2008), the project deals with its causes and consequences. At the causes level it promotes entrepreneurship and advocacy among students, teachers and parents. Social entrepreneurship is a strategy for job and wealth creation, promoting social capital too. At the consequence level it addresses the nutritional and emotional problems related to the economic crisis that are affecting the children's wellbeing. Growing inequality (Wilkinson & Pickett, 2009) and the economic crisis are connected to malnourishment and obesity, and to emotional problems (Sindic de Greuges, 2013).

Occupational therapy: creating healthy, inclusive and sustainable communities

The author defines occupational therapy as the art and science of empowering people (groups, communities) to develop a full life project through the development of meaningful occupations. Its purpose is to create healthy, sustainable, and inclusive communities where everyone participates as a citizen with full rights experiencing wellbeing (Simó Algado, 2015).

Occupational therapy is essentially cooperating with people, groups and communities to be able to have control over their lives and to develop a meaningful life project (Simó Algado & Guzman, 2014). A life project relates to the capacity to develop an existence coherent with the person's values that fulfils his/her human development and vital expectations, promoting wellbeing and social inclusion.

A central belief in occupational therapy is that engaging in meaningful occupations promotes health and wellbeing (Ikiugu & Pollard, 2015). The associated concept of occupational justice maintains that all people should have access to occupations of meaning, enabling them to enjoy life and flourish (Townsend & Wilcock, 2004). Access to meaningful occupation can be seen as a human right (Guajardo & Simó Algado, 2010). Lack of meaning may translate into depression, aggression or addiction (Frankl, 1964), some of the major problems affecting our societies.

Community-based approaches, health promotion, culture, citizenship and entrepreneurship are key aspects in the intervention and each will be discussed in continuation. The ability to create and coordinate alliances, to be innovative and resilient, to have a complex understanding of the situation and to integrate intervention with research to develop an evidence based practice are key competences for occupational therapists working at the community arena.

A community-based occupational therapy sensible to the social determinants of health

'Suffering, more than admiration, makes us think.' Leonardo Boff.

As a profession we must think and act to alleviate this suffering in order to be a really useful and relevant profession for society. Our greatest challenge as occupational therapists is to create healthy, sustainable, and inclusive communities where everyone participates as a citizen with full-rights, thus enabled to experience wellbeing. It is essential to promote health (OMS, 1997) addressing the social determinants of health (CSDH, 2008). Occupational therapy has been focused too much on individual interventions, when often the context promotes occupational injustices. As a profession we have not given enough attention to realities such as poverty, with the important exception of Competences for Poverty Reduction (van Bruggen, Kantartzis & Rowan, 2010), a multi professional congress under the umbrella of ENOTHE led by van Bruggen. Poverty, unemployment and job precariousness are important social determinants of health that occupational therapy must address.

Sen (2000) defines poverty as the inability to control one's own life due to the lack of capabilities. Occupational therapy is based in a capacitation science (Townsend & Polajatko, 2007), as it aims at empowering individuals, groups and communities.

Following Sen's definition we can say that occupational therapy can deal directly with poverty. Poverty predisposes to occupational dysfunction, being directly related to occupational deprivation and occupational injustice.

A process of individualization (Beck, 2003) and social atomism (Bauman, 2005a), the promotion of individual isolation, is destroying community ties. It is necessary to recover the pronoun *we* (Sennett, 2006). This reality reinforces the importance of developing community based occupational therapy interventions. As occupational therapists we have to increase our presence in the community, not only to develop 'projects for' but also to develop 'projects with' the communities (Sanz, 2012). It is important to move from 'therapeutic' institutions to the natural scenarios of the populations. The core of the profession lies in the relationship between the person and the community, and what they do (want to do or need to do) in their environment within a framework of health, wellbeing and occupational justice (van Bruggen et al, 2012).

Health promotion and education

Although occupational therapists more typically offer preventive services to individuals presenting with specific risks or disabilities in their clinical practice, they may also play a broader role in promoting the health and wellness of groups, communities, and whole populations by developing and implementing interventions designed for people without any specific illness or disabilities (Filiatrault et al, 2015).

Schools are an area of intervention for the promotion of wellbeing and occupational participation. The author developed projects for the promotion of mental health, preventing trauma related to war, in Guatemala (Simó Algado & Burgman 2005; Simó Algado, 1997) and Kosovo (Simó Algado & Estuardo, 2004; Simó Algado et al, 2002). The interventions were located in the schools empowering children, teachers and parents.

Failure in school is often related to social exclusion as it jeopardizes the student's subsequent inclusion in work (Escardibul, 2013). Occupational therapy intervention has been mostly focused on addressing functional diversity and disabilities in the school system. School failure can be caused by emotional disorders too. Experiencing situations of poverty, family dislocation and stress affects the mental and nutritional wellbeing and the occupational performance of children in the school. It is vital to ensure the emotional and nutritional wellbeing of children addressing the sources of poverty such as unemployment (CSDH, 2008).

A collaborative approach with children, parents and teachers to establish partnerships with the public, private and Third sector is required when providing community-based occupational therapy to educationally and health at risk children.

Occupational therapy and culture

Occupational behaviour is always an environmental behaviour; occupation is the dialogue between human beings with their environment. Culture is a key dimension in our profession, particularly when we want to develop community-based interventions in schools marked for their cultural diversity.

Kymlicka (1996, p.112) defines the culture of a society as

'that which provides its members a meaningful form of life across the full range of human activities, including social, educational, recreational, and economic life, bringing public and private spheres.'

According to Bauman (2009) there are two main ways of understanding culture. One generated the idea of culture as the activity of the free spirit. It is the seat of creativity, of invention and of self-transcendence. The other raises culture as an instrument of continuity, in the service of the social order. The first conception understands culture as ability to resist the rules. It is *poiesis*, art and creation. For the second, it means an aggregate or consistent system of pressure resting on sanctions, of internalized values and norms, which guarantee the preservation of tradition. So Bauman (2009) concluded that the culture is both an agent of disorder and an instrument of order. It is both a space of creativity and a regulatory policy framework.

Western occupational therapists need to be aware that Western thought always has related with other cultures from the position of discoverer (Sousa, 2005). It is necessary to develop a culturally safe occupational therapy practice recovering culture as a creative activity of the free spirit that allows resistence of unfair rules and situations. Intervention situated outside the cultural context can become irrelevant, or an agent of oppression that will colonize and even marginalize people (Iwama & Simó Algado, 2008).

To develop projects with communities in a safe and fair manner, we need to understand that culture and diversity are key concepts of our interventions introducing culturally meaningful occupations (Simó Algado 2016; Simó Algado & Burgman, 2005).

Cosmopolitan citizenship

In the face of racism and ethnocentrism occupational therapy can promote a cosmopolitan citizenship. To achieve an inclusive and tolerant society the best strategy is to educate for it (Cortina, 2005). Cosmopolitanism refers to the idea of a city without walls (Peña, 2010). Moral and political cosmopolitism establishes a series of rights and moral obligations between all human beings. This moral community is built on the basis of the elimination of discrimination and suffering (Habermas, 1999). A cosmopolitan citizen shows interest in thinking critically about global issues, with awareness of their mutual interdependence with others in the world around them. Such a person has a sense of citizenship, which is both rooted locally and situated in the world through complex forms and identities. The cosmopolitan citizen shows respect for diversity and reacts with indignation to exclusion (Paz Abril, 2007). Cosmopolitan citizens are aware of their obligations and are responsible for their actions. They are aware of their rights too. As occupational therapists we have to recover the concientization role proposed by Freire (2009); to be aware of the right to have rights (Benhabib, 2005). Occupational therapists can develop an advocacy role with the community members to denounce the injustices they are suffering and to develop action to confront them by political and social activism.

Occupational justice and social entrepreneurship

Occupational justice has been defined as the promotion of a social and economic change to ensure access to meaningful occupations (Whiteford & Townsend, 2011). This change requires an understanding of the current economic system and actively looking for or creating alternatives. A major part of the world is immersed in a capitalistic system that primarily seeks the accumulation of wealth, creating huge global inequity. Oxfam (2016) denounces the fact that the 62 richest people in the world own as much as the poorest half of the world's population. A growing part of the world population is being excluded from participating in the economic system. Unemployment changes its meaning from a temporary to a definitive state (Bauman, 2005b). Unemployment is one problem causing poverty and mental health suffering (CSDH, 2008), job precariousness is the other (Beck, 2000). As occupational therapists we need to work with employers or create meaningful jobs for the people as work is the main guarantee of social inclusion and a key aspect in adults' life projects. At the same time we need to be aware that there will be less work so as occupational therapists we have the challenge to find alternatives.

As occupational therapists we must explore alternatives such as social entrepreneurship, one economic strategy that aims to generate social benefits. Social entrepreneurs are people looking for innovative solutions to most pressing health, social and ecological problems. At the Universitat de Vic we are leading a master's programme in social entrepreneurship. We have the honour of working with the guidance of Nobel Peace Prize winner Mohammed Yunus. We are part of the Yunus academy. In Yunus' understanding the benefits produced by social enterprises must be reinvested in the enterprise, rather than as dividends distributed for profit (Yunus, 2005). Other interesting paths to explore are the economy of common good or the *décroissance sereine*. The economy of the common good (Felber, 2012) advocates for an alternative economic model. It calls for working towards the common good and cooperation instead of profit-orientation and competition, which lead to greed and uncontrolled growth. The *décroissance sereine* (Latouche, 2009) proposes the controlled decline of economic output, with the aim of establishing a new equilibrium relationship between humans and nature, but also among human beings themselves.

The project

The Sinia School is situated on the outskirts of Vic, a city of 45,000 inhabitants located in the northeast of Barcelona. In the city there are currently more than 80 nationalities, with 24% of the population being of immigrant origin (Idescat, 2015). The city context is marked by racism. Until recently the racist political party *Plataforma per Catalunya* was the second political force in the city council. At the time of writing, Islamophobia had increased since the attacks in France, Belgium and Germany during 2016.

The school was located in the neighbourhood of Remei, which had a greater percentage of immigrant people than the rest of the city. The director of the school reported that 95% children were inmmigrants or the children of immigrants. Its pupils share 25 nationalities with 17 languages present in the school. Unfortunately this cultural asset was not valued by a major part of the population; some parents refused to bring their children to the school due to the high percentage of immigrants.

The economic crisis has seriously affected the neighbourhood. 49.5% of Sinia School's children were at risk of poverty. Remei's health centre was concerned about the nutritional problems manifested by the children.

The Sinia School contacted the author through the city council social worker for support to address its main problems. This contact led to a first meeting with the director, the head of studies, a teachers' representative as well as the social worker. During this meeting they discussed the main problems that affected the school. This was complemented by a participatory diagnosis with teachers and parents.

The economic situation seriously affected families' welfare. Some lacked the resources to pay for gas or electricity. Other families live in 'patera' flats, where several families share illegally overcrowded accomodation to be able to afford the rent. These issues also impact on the emotional wellbeing of the children and therefore affect their academic performance.

After these meetings the author wrote a first draft of the project proposal. It was based on a review of the international scientific literature and the author's previous experiences. This first draft was validated with the school team, preparing a final draft in collaboration during a series of meetings. The project was structured in five interrelated programs:

Box 1. The programs of the project

The first phase of the project was developed between September 2016 and June 2017.

1. Emotional wellbeing
Goal:
- To promote the children's emotional wellbeing.
- To enable the teachers and parents as mental health promoters.

Actions:
- All the teachers of the school will receive 12 hours theoretical training and then 8 hours practical training working with all the children (6-12 years old) with the supervision of the first author, an occupational therapist.
- A group of parents selected by the school will receive 8 hours of training, followed up with 4 hours of supervision sessions.

Gestalt therapy, art therapy and occupational therapy are the main theoretical foundations of this workshop led by occupational therapists.

2. Nutritional wellbeing

Goal:
- To ensure children's' nutritional wellbeing.

Actions:
- To screen for the nutritional state of the children.
- To create a living food lab to develop culinary workshops with children and their parents. In this workshop their culinary knowledge will be recognised and will

be complemented to assure the best nutrition for the families. Two groups will be created, for children (6-9 years old and 10-12 years old) and their parents. Duration: 50 hours (each workshop).

- To create a horticultural garden in the school with the participation of children (6-12 years old), teachers, parents and community members. Duration: 120 hours.

This workshop will be conducted by nutritionist from the UVic-UCC.

3. Culture

Goal:
- To promote the value of the richness of the cultural diversity that enables the school to promote multicultural citizenship.
- To ensure universal access to extra scholar activities.

Actions:
- Storytelling workshop: recollection of stories with the children (6-7-8 years) and their families. Creation and publication of new stories. Duration: 80 hours.
- Theatre Workshop: to train the teachers in social theatre, known as Theatre of the Oppressed (Boal, 2009) to create a play where the children (9-10 years) will explore their social reality. Duration: 80 hours.
- Graffiti and comic workshop: creation of a graffiti group and comics where children (11-12 years) explore their experiences. Duration: 80 hours.
- Gospel music and batukada workshops: These workshops will be offered to all the children (6-12 years) in the school as extra scholar activitiy. Batukada is a form of Brazilian music, which is a kind of samba with lots of drums. Duration: 80 hours.

These workshops will be developed by occupational therapists in collaboration with well-known illustrators, actors, urban writers, and musicians from the region.

4. Cosmopolitan citizenship

Goal:
- To promote a cosmopolitan citizenship through which all are aware of their rights and obligations.
- To advocate for the rights of the children, parents and community members.
- To promote political and social activism in the school and neighbourhhod.

Actions:
- To develop awareness workshops inspired by the Pedagogy of the oppressed (Freire, 2009) with children (10-12 years old), parents and community members.
- To develop the campaign "I have rights and I have duties as a citizen". Through this campaign the children will demonstrate their contribution to the life of the city and also revindicate their rights.
- To facilitate the participation of the parents in associations developing political activism.

This workshop will be developed by occupational therapists in collaboration with the teachers. Duration: 50 hours.

5. Social entrepreneurship

Goal:
- To spread an entrepreneurship culture among the children and parents.

Actions:
- To develop entrepreneurial workshops among the children (12 years old).
- To train groups of parents in the entrepreneurship.
- To identify potential productive projects.
- To look for funding for the follow up to the projects.

These workshops will be developed by occupational therapists in collaboration with experts in social entrepreneurship. Duration: 80 hours.

Philosophically, the project is based in a holistic, humanistic philosophy, with meaningful occupations as the core of our interventions. Theoretically, it is based on the Canadian Model of Occupational Performance and Engagement (CMOP-E) (Townsend & Polajatko, 2007). The Canadian Model of Client Centred Enablement (CMCE) is a useful tool to guide our client centred interventions (Townsend & Polajatko, 2007). Reflections from the Participatory Occupational Justice Framework (POJF) (Whiteford & Townsend, 2011) have also been included.

The project can be considered an occupational reconstruction (Frank & Austin, 2015) as it was originated by the teachers and the parents themselves in order to transform a problematic social situation related to poverty, inequity and forced migrations. Needs have been identified from a participatory diagnosis. The children, parents and teachers have an active role in the project based in a capacitation philosophy. Transformation takes place by engaging mindfully in a collective occupation within a concentrated time frame (the first phase lasts one year) in order to fulfill an articulated social change. The first outcomes expected are to improve the nutritional and emotional wellbeing of the children, to increase their entrepreneurial skills and to assure a universal access to extra scholar activities promoting their artistic/ human development. It is a collage of meaningful and interelated occupations mainly based in art media (such as music, painting, theater or storytelling).

Engagement in the project is based on parents and teachers' determination to build a better present and future for their children. Social justice and human rights/ dignity are values guiding the project. Related knowledge from Community Based Rehabilitation (Sanz, 2012), community development, education, psychology, sociology, anthropology, politics, art, ecology and entrepreneurship have been taken into consideration.

Box 2. Applying the enabling principles and the CMCE

The 5 principles of CMOP-E can be applied to the project:
- **Client's participation:** developing participatory analysis, designing a common project and starting capacitation processes.
- **Vision of possibility**: creating a healthier, sustainable and inclusive society.

- **Change**: ensuring educational occupational success for children in order to guarantee their social inclusion.
- **Justice, diversity and equity:** fighting against occupational injustice in education; valuing and promoting cultural diversity; promoting equity supplying free services for populations without access.

The competences of the CMCE can be applied:

- Adapting the occupational therapy intervention to the community needs and context.
- Advocating for children's and parent's rights.
- Coaching teachers and parents as mental health promoters and entrepreneurs.
- Collaborating with local NGO's and enterprises in order to achieve funding.
- Consulting parents, teachers, children and mental health and nutritional experts.
- Coordinating with the university, the school, the local mental health centre, and the city council.
- Designing an emotional promotion project.
- Educating children as cosmopolitan citizens.
- Engaging teachers, parents and children in the project.
- Specializing in the development of community interventions.
- Sharing power with clients through the capacitation process as mental health promoters and researchers.

The art of partnership

A partnership was established with the third sector, public sector, and private sector (Tennyson, 2011).

Third Sector. UVic-UCC's participation in the project was important. Apart from my coordinator role, students were actively involved in the project through the service learning (SL) educational strategy. I had previous experience developing SL projects for occupational therapy, for example developing a social inclusion project for mental health survivors and for teenagers at risk (Simó Algado, 2013). SL seeks educational excellence at the same time that it provides a service to the community, from a reality-based learning perspective.

Sixteen third year students from the inclusive education module in the occupational therapy programme developed a pilot project in mental health promotion with two classes from the school. At first the students visited the school and the director informed them about the situation. The students had two classes of inclusive education during the week. During the first class, they prepared the session with the first author's supervision. During the second session they led the sessions with the supervision of the first author and support from the schoolteachers.

Two PhD students, one of whom was a teacher from la Sinia School, developed their research based on this project, ensuring human resources during the next 3 years. They early on developed the participatory analysis with the parents and the teachers, which consisted of a SWOT analysis (strengths, weaknesses, opportunities and threats).

At the same time the development of a nutritional screening project and the living food lab was led by the nutrition program at UVic.

Public sector. Vic city council agreed to support the project. The local mental health foundation Osona Mental Health was added to the partnership. The psychologist treating the children, who had already revealed the mental health problems at the school, was invited to be part of the team.

Private sector. A competitive award from the *Obra Social La Caixa Foundation* secured a 25000 euros grant. At the same time we negotiated with two NGOs and with local enterprises through their corporate social responsibility (CSR) obligations. CSR engages in actions that appear to further some social good, beyond the interests of the firm.

The research project

I was the director of the two PhD students mentioned above, one of who was a teacher at the school. The project was informed by participatory action research (PAR). PAR is a form of collaborative research particularly concerned with power inequities of marginalized communities. With this approach, occupational therapists can work with clients and communities to address issues of access, inclusion, equity and collaboration in practice and research (Cockburn, 2002). The project sought to improve the social context using a critical paradigm. The research questions were agreed with the PhD students and the school board. During the research process children were to have an active role in developing participatory techniques.

Box 3. A mixed methods research proposal

The research methodology uses mixed methods, since it combines qualitative and quantitative research. The first part will be qualitative, with the goal of creating new knowledge about the situation under research.

- To develop a participatory analysis. Focus groups have been developed with the participation of teachers, parents and experts. Focus groups with experts in education, emotional wellbeing, culture, etc. will also develop.
- To generate knowledge from the children's perception. Participatory methods such as photo voice will be developed with the children to learn about their own perceptions of their situation.

With this knowledge, plus the review of international relevant literature a program how to promote emotional wellbeing will be created.

The second phase will be quantitative with the goal to establish the effectiveness of the intervention. An experimental and control groups will be developed. Pre and post evaluation will be developed with the two groups from the school. If the project shows benefits the control group will receive the intervention after 3 months.

Discussion

'Human action is our capacity to create miracles'. Hanna Arendt.

Occupational therapy must abandon the security of the institutions to become immersed in communities, as they are the real scenarios of people. This is a key factor if as a profession we want to deal with the social determinants of health promoting occupational justice. The process of empowering communities can be a powerful transformation tool for enabling health promotion. Children, teachers and parents are great resources for our interventions, among others. The occupational performance of children at school must be ensured in order to achieve academic success that lead to good job inclusion in the society. Failure in education contributes to social exclusion. Poor occupational performance can be related to serious emotional and nutritional problems and the problems related to the context characterized by poverty, unemployment, racism and stress.

As has already been discussed culture is a basic contextual dimension (Simó Algado, 2016; Iwama & Simó Algado 2008) profoundly linked with the construction of meaning (Kymlicka, 1996). Occupational therapists must understand culture in order to find with the clients really meaningful occupations. In the project culture has been understood as the activity of the free spirit, a powerful tool to challenge an established order that perpetuates inequality. It is poiesis, our capacity to create a more fair, inclusive and sustainable society (Bauman, 2009). Meaningful occupations are the soul of the intervention. The mental health promotion program is based on play. Gospel singing, batukada (music percussion originally from Brazil), storytelling, and theatre have been identified with the school community as meaningful occupations for the children incorporating the richness of their culture.

Citizenship and human rights are key concepts for occupational therapy. We can promote a cosmopolitan citizenship from a human rights driven profession (Guajardo & Simó Algado, 2010). In a scenario characterised by the reduction of social rights, it is basic to create political awareness à la Freire (2009). Children and parents will develop the awareness that they have rights and duties as citizens. Claiming rights and empowering communities are crucial in this process developing the advocacy role of occupational therapy.

To deal with the social determinants of heath (CSDH, 2008) implies to deal with realities such as poverty, unemployment or job precariousness. Social entrepreneurship is a powerful tool that occupational therapist can use to promote occupational justice. It is needed to promote economic change assuring access to meaningful job opportunities. It is important to spread an entrepreneurial culture looking for innovative and creative solutions to contemporary challenges.

The art of partnership and resilience are key competences for occupational therapists, among others; to create partnerships, creating alliances with the public, private and the Third Sector (civil society). To be resilient (Cyrulnik, 2002), resisting the difficulties and frustrations that appear during the process is vital for the success of the interventions.

Our last goal is to create healthy, sustainable, and inclusive communities where everyone participates as a citizen with full-rights experiencing wellbeing (Simó Algado, 2015).

Further information

Since the writing of this chapter the project has been implemented. You can find additional information about the project at:
http://www.sentx100.net/la-sinia-vic/ Catalan

General video:
https://youtu.be/QIh_wCFkaQg

Emotional wellbeing workshop:
https://youtu.be/l8fRGkS_XJk

Theatre workshop:
https://www.youtube.com/watch?v=EpMRhZ06L3M

Urban art workshop:
https://www.youtube.com/watch?v=HX2-ZDaMmok

Oriental art workshop:
https://www.youtube.com/watch?v=r9JZw1jAdMU

Preparing final presentation for parents:
https://www.youtube.com/watch?v=fs2EVdUzPyQ
https://www.youtube.com/watch?v=rMm87umtt7U

References

Bauman, Z. (2005a) *Tiempos Líquidos. Vivir en una época de incertidumbre.* Barcelona: Tusquets

Bauman, Z. (2005b) *Vidas Desperdiciadas. La modernidad y sus parias.* Barcelona: Paidós

Bauman, Z. (2009) *La Cultura Como Praxis.* Barcelona: Paidós

Beck, U. and Beck-Gernsheim, E. (2003) *La Individualización.* Barcelona: Paidós

Beck, U. (2000) *Un Nuevo Mundo Feliz.* Barcelona. Paidós

Benhabib, S. (2005) *Los Derechos De Los Otros.* Barcelona: Gedisa

Boal, A. (2009) *El Teatro Del Oprimido.* Madrid: Alba Editorial

Castells, M. (2005) Global governance and global politics. *Political Science and Politics,* 38, 1, 9-15

Cockburn, L. and Trentham, B. (2002). Participatory action research: Integrating community occupational therapy practice and research. *Canadian Journal of Occupational Therapy,* 69, 20-30

Cortina, A. (2008) *Ética Aplicada Y Democracia Radical.* Madrid: Tecnos

CSDH (2008) *Closing the Gap in a Generation: Health equity through action on the social determinants of health.* Geneva: World Health Organization

Cyrulnik, B. (2002). *Los Patitos Feos.* Barcelona: Editorial Gedisa

Escardidul, J. (2013). Fracaso escolar y paro juvenil en España. *Revista de Pedagogía de la Universidad de Salamanca,* 19, 27-46

European Anti Poverty Network EAPN (2014). *Dossier Pobreza De EAPN De España.* [Accessed 14 September 2016 at http://www.eapn.es/ARCHIVO/documentos/dossier_pobreza.pdf]

Felber, C. (2012) *Economía Del Bien Común*. Bilbao: Deusto

Filiatrault, J., Parisien, M., Sullivan, A., Richard, L. and Pinard, C. (2015) Prevention and health promotion in occupational therapy: From concepts to interventions. *International Handbook Of Occupational Therapy Interventions, (2nd edition)* (pp. 837-848)

Frank, G. and Austin, B. (2015) Theorising social transformation in Occupational Science: The American civil rights movement and South African struggle against apartheid as occupational reconstructions. *South African Journal of Occupational Therapy*, 45,1, 11-20

Frankl, V. (1964) *El Hombre en Busca de Sentido*. Barcelona: Herder

Freire, P. (2009) *Pedagogía del Oprimido*. Madrid: Siglo XXI

Guajardo, A. and Simó Algado, S. (2010) Una terapia ocupacional basada en los derechos humanos. *TOG*, 7, 12, 1-25 [Accessed 12 June 2016 at http://www.revistatog.com/num12/pdfs/maestros.pdf]

Habermas, J. (1999) *La Inclusión Del Otro*. Barcelona: Paidós

Idescat (2015) Instituto de Estadística de Cataluña. [Accessed 15 September 2016 at http://www.idescat.cat/es/]

Ikiugu, M. and Pollard, N. (2015) *Meaningful Living Through Occupation: Occupation-based intervention strategies for occupational therapists and scientists.* London: Whiting & Birch

Iwama, M., Simó Algado, S. and Kapanadze, M. (2008) En busca de una Terapia Ocupacional culturalmente relevante. *TOG*, 5,8,1-29 [Accessed 12 June 2016 at http://www.revistatog.com/num8/pdfs/maestros.pdf]

Kymlicka, W. (1996) *Ciudadanía Multicultural*. Barcelona: Paidós

Latouche, S. (2009) *Petit Tractat Sobre el Decreixement Serè*. Valencia: Tres i Quatre

Navarro, V. (2006) *El Subdesarrollo Social en España*. Barcelona: Anagrama

Organización Mundial de la Salud OMS (1997) *Declaración de Yakarta*. [Accessed 12 June 2016 at http://www.who.int/hpr/NPH/docs/jakarta_declaration_sp.pdf]

Oxfam (2016) *An Economy For The 1%*. [Accessed 10 September 2016 at http://policy-practice.oxfam.org.uk/publications/an-economy-for-the-1-how-privilege-and-power-in-the-economy-drive-extreme-inequ-592643]

de Paz Abril, D. (2007) *Escuelas y Educación para la Ciudadanía Global*. Barcelona: Intermon Oxfam

Peña, J. (2010) *La Ciudad sin Murallas*. Mataró: El Viejo topo

Pollard, N., Sakellariou, D. and Kronenberg F. (2008) *A Political Practice Of Occupational Therapy*. Edinburgh: Churchill Livingstone

Real Academia Española (2015) Diccionario. [Accessed 12 September 2016 at http://www.rae.es]

Sanz, S. (2012) Reflexiones y aprendizajes en torno a la rbc. *TOG*, monog 5, 206-226. [Accessed 12 Septebmer 2016 at http://www.revistatog.com/mono/num5/comunidad.pdf]

Sen, A. (2000) *Desarrollo y Libertad*. Barcelona: Planeta

Sennett, R. (2006) *La Corrosión del Carácter*. Barcelona: Anagrama

Simó Algado, S. (2016) Terapia ocupacional, cultura y diversidad. *Cadernos de terapia ocupacional*, 24, 1, 163-171 [Accessed 25 September 2016 at http://www.cadernosdeterapiaocupacional.ufscar.br/index.php/cadernos/article/view/1309]

Simó Algado, S. (2015) Una terapia ocupacional desde un paradigma critico. *TOG*, 7,7, 25-41 [Accessed 14 September 2016 at http://www.revistatog.com/mono/num7/critico.pdf]

Simó Algado, S. (2004) The return of the corn man. in F. Kronenberg, S. Simó Algado and N. Pollard (Eds.) Occupational Therapy Without Borders: Learning from the spirit of survivors.

Oxford: Elsevier's Science

Simó Algado, S. and Burgman, I. (2005) Children survivors of war. In F. Kronenberg, S. Simó Algado and N. Pollard (Eds.) Occupational Therapy Without Borders: Learning from the spirit of survivors. Toronto: Elsevier Churchill Livingstone (pp.205-217.)

Simó Algado, S., Ginesta, X. and San Eugenio, J. (2013) Aprendizaje Servicio Universitario: creando empleo a partir de la emprendeduría social. *Historia y Comunicación Social*, 18, Nov, 627-638

Simó Algado, S., and Guzmán, S. (2014) Construyendo proyectos de vida con personas supervivientes de enfermedad mental. *TOG*, 11, 9 [Accessed 14 September 2016 at http://www.revistatog.com/num19/pdfs/maestros.pdf]

Simó Algado, S. and Mehta, N. (2002) Occupational therapy intervention with children survivors of war. *Canadian Journal of Occupational Therapy*, 69,4, 205-217

Simó Algado, S., Rodriguez Gregori, J. and Egan, M. (1997) Spirituality in a refugee camp. *Canadian Journal of Occupational Therapy*, 61, 88-94

Simó Algado, S. and Townsend, E. (2015) Ecosocial occupational therapy. *British Journal of Occupational Therapy*, 78,3, 182-186

Sindic de greuges (2013) *Informe Sobre la Malnutrición en Cataluña*. [Accessed 12 June 2016 at http://www.sindic.cat/site/unitFiles/3505/Informe%20malnutricio%20infantil%20castella.pdf]

Sousa Santos, B. (2005) *El Milenio Huérfano. Ensayos para una nueva cultura política*. Madrid: Editorial Trotta

Tennyson, R. (2011) *The Partnering Toolbook*. [Accessed 12 June 2016 at http://thepartneringinitiative.org/publications/toolbook-series/the-partnering-toolbook/]

Townsend E. and Polajatko H. (2007) *Enabling Occupation II: Advancing an Occupational Therapy Vision for Health, Well-being & Justice through Occupation*. Toronto: CAOT Publications

Townsend, A. and Wilcock, A. (2004) Occupational justice and client-centred practice: A dialogue. *Canadian Journal of Occupational Therapy* 71, 2, 75-87

Townsend, E. and Whiteford, G. (2005) A participatory occupational justice framework: Population-based processes of practice. in F. Kronenberg, S. Simo Algado and N. Pollard (Eds.) *Occupational Therapy without Borders: Learning from the spirit of survivors*. Toronto: Elsevier Churchill Livingstone

van Bruggen, H., Kantartzis, S. and Rowan, S. (Eds.) (2010) *Competences for poverty reduction*, COPORE. Amsterdam: ENOTHE

van Bruggen, H., Rivas Quarneti, N., Viana Moldes, I., Kapanadze, M. and Simó Algado, S. (2012) *Master of Occupational Therapy*. Hanneke van Bruggen. TOG, Coruna, Spain. [accessed 29 November 2016 at www.revistatog.com/num16pdfs/maestro2.pdf]

Wilkinson G. and Pickett, K. (2009) *The Spirit Level*. London: Allen Lane

Yunus, M. (2005) *Hacia un Mundo sin Pobreza*. Santiago de Chile: Andrés Bello

Chapter 9
Building inclusive communities through occupation

Miyuki Minato

Working in the community is meaningful for people with mental illness (Villotti et al, 2012; Leufstadius et al, 2008; Haertl & Minato, 2006; Rudman et al, 2000). Over the past 60 years in Japan, workplaces for people with disabilities, including those with mental illness, have divided into general employment and sheltered workshops. In fact, Japan's constitution specifies that all citizens have the right to work; however, support for employment is initiated only after evaluating whether people with disabilities are able to do the same work as people without disabilities. This chapter reports on the Work Sharing Employment Support Project which is aimed at promoting health for people with mental illness and promoting inclusive communities (Minato, 2014) based in the occupational science understanding of the significance of occupation, including its impacts on the health and social context (Townsend, 1997; Zemke & Clark, 1996).

The Work Sharing Employment Support Project actively endeavors to increase access to local community employment for people with mental illness through designing individualized work opportunities. By applying the knowledge gained from occupational science related to occupation and health to employment support for those with mental illness, this project has created many options for such individuals. The project has been working with Aichi Medical College, Owari-Chubu Employment and the Assisted Living Center for People with Disabilities in Aichi prefecture to create choices for people with mental illness who want to work in the community and to support mainstream employment for all clients (Minato et al, 2016).

The Work Sharing Project also revealed the importance of university leadership in local communities' development (Minato, 2013; Minato, 2009). To meet local community needs, Kibi International University (KIU) Work Sharing Project in Okayama prefecture and Owari-Chubu Work Sharing Project in Aichi prefecture extended efforts toward such leadership. In 2005, the KIU project commenced after evaluation of the needs of a local nonprofit organization (NPO) for people with mental illness. After evaluating a local employment support center's needs for people with mental illness, the Owari-Chubu project began in 2015. Both these projects aimed to enable inclusion in the community through work.

Breaking away from an exclusive policy

For people with mental illness, working in a community is both a need and a right. Although Japan's constitution secures the right to work for all citizens, many people with mental illness have no opportunities to work in inclusive work environments.

According to a Ministry of Health, Labor and Welfare statistical report (fiscal year 2013), Japan has 3,200,000 people of working age with mental health problems but only 48,000 general employers of people with mental illness (Ministry of Health Labor and Welfare, 2013). Those who obtain work through social welfare services for the disabled, such as sheltered workshops, number approximately 80,000. Japanese government policy firmly divides workplaces for people with mental illness into those offering inclusive employment and sheltered workshops. Although many people with mental illness want to work in inclusive workplaces, merely 4.6% of the clients attending sheltered workshops annually make the transition to working in inclusive workplaces (Ministry of Health Labor and Welfare, 2015). Even for those people who want to work with support the preparatory training is conducted in other places to the sheltered workshops. Since they do not have access to work in general workplaces, most people do not have the opportunity to find more suitable work or make choices about their employment. The process of such support in Japan results in weakening the power which leads to inclusive communities.

Despite evidence that working does not necessarily lead to a recurrence of mental illness (Becker & Drake, 2004), staff members who support people with mental health issues to work tend to retain a simplistic assumption that work is contraindicated. This belief is used to justify insufficient support; moreover, it increases the expectation that support will be insufficient.

In 2005, the Work Sharing Project started to create community based work opportunities for people with mental illness. Sheltered workshop clients and staff members, along with university researchers, developed the practice of the project by collaborating with various job partners - companies, institutions, and the area's administration. The Work Sharing Project aims to make the inclusion of people with mental illness in employment a reality through designing meaningful work for each client. The project focuses on building inclusive occupational opportunities to work in an integrated community environment.

Meaningful Work Design Model

The Work Sharing Project has aimed for clients to have meaningful opportunities for working in a general environment from the beginning. The intervention approach was planned and based on the Meaningful Work Design Model (Minato, 2014). This model focuses on the following elements:

* creating choices for work in inclusive environments,
* requesting that clients actively select and design their method of working,
* constructing situations that positively support clients' needs,
* focusing on meaningful and subjective experiences for clients,
* supporting clients' employment goals,
* and assisting clients' in balancing their mental and physical energy.

This project proposes sharing work in communities instead of providing support for employment that priorities training and preparation in an exclusive (closed) social environment. Clients who were working at sheltered workshops realized that they could work at general, inclusive workplaces by choosing separately for one day 2–4 hours of work from choices in the community. The project has applied knowledge focused on health promotion through work for people with mental illness (Minato, 2010).

The World Federation of Occupational Therapists (WFOT, 2006) issued a clear statement regarding strategies for social action to appropriately consider justice and occupational rights. To support the development of occupational science, the WFOT also expressed its recognition of the value of occupational therapy derived from occupational science. There is a need for occupational science research to address the considerable societal problems that prevent the realisation of occupational potential and develop strategies to meet the needs that will be evidenced. The Work Sharing Project was initiated from such ideas and aims at promoting health and inclusive communities for people with mental illness. Herein, the author reports on the Work Sharing Project that actively attempts to increase access to local community employment for people with mental illness. The project emphasizes clients' opinions concerning their work opportunities, including their perceptions of their preferred working conditions and participation. The project also emphasizes balancing one's energy, accomplishing tasks, and achieving progress in meaningful work by designing the work.

This project has generated some job opportunities in the general environment, such as washing bottles before recycling in a cleaning company, printing handouts for lectures at the university, cleaning wheelchairs in the geriatric hospital, and carrying out reception duties at the institute.

Participants with mental illness have worked continuously in the community and have been provided with choices in, for instance, the structure of their occupation (e.g. frequency, hours, location, and tasks), degree of flexibility (e.g. pace and task complexity), and degree of change (e.g. scheduled times and tasks). To meet the diverse employment needs of people with mental illness in the local community, a framework was needed to provide a varied range of jobs. Moreover, a conceptual framework was required for accumulating knowledge and skills for employment support for people with mental illness.

This project planned its employment support from the perspective of the 'Meaningful Work Design Model', a practice based on the idea of occupational science (Figure 1). The model focuses on the following: 1) choices that bring flexibility to work in general environments, 2) clients' meaningful selection and design of their method of working, 3) situations that positively support clients' needs, 4) clients' employment goals, and 5) clients' management of mental and physical energy.

This model's assumptions are as follows: 1) Designing meaningful work will be attained when flexible choices are available to clients, and clients choose work suitable for the achievement of a target relevant to their commitment and to a lifestyle relevant to appropriate management of their energy. 2) When clients' say 'I want to work,' that need will be affirmed. Staff will get to know clients and promote actual employment through designing meaningful work or promoting an idea of work. For example, a local resident might gradually understand the importance of sharing work and probably offer work opportunities to clients once they have understood the need for choices based in the community - for instance, support related to time, frequency, job/task difficulty as well as understanding of the task, and opportunities for training. 3) The staff will gradually support the clients who want to work in making choices about work and work places independently and then carrying the work out themselves.

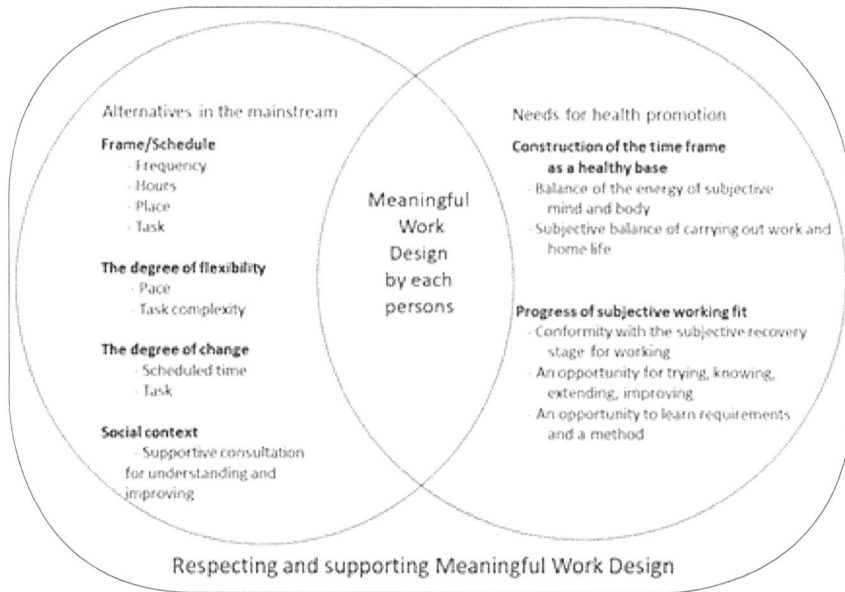

Figure 1. Meaningful Work Design Model

Practice of Meaningful Work Design Model

In Japan, there are insufficient alternatives to work for people with mental illness, and goal-directed approaches for achieving employment results are unknown. Even if an individual's preparation and training is good and support is offered, the minimum time in supported work has to be set at 20 hours of work a week at an early stage in order for a person with mental illness to take advantage of the step up employment incentive offered by the Ministry of Health, Labour and Welfare in Japan (Ministry of Health, Labor and Welfare, 2016). Therefore, many clients have to forgo working. As already mentioned, only 3.6% of the clients from sheltered workshops move on to employment. Therefore the need to promote and develop a concept of meaningful work in Japan led to the proposal of this project and the creation of work opportunities, education for employers about developing work opportunities, and the evaluation of clients' working needs.

One of the intervention's main purposes was to create a tool, a questionnaire, with which to elicit the development of a specific task which clients will find meaningful. Questions were created based on occupational knowledge about health and occupation (Minato, 2003), and not only clients but also their family and the staff had to review the method of working from the viewpoint of health (Table 1). Using this tool, clients, families and staff had the opportunity to review health issues and help improve methods of healthy working based on individual targets and energy levels. Through this review, a high number of family and staff members learned about the positive effects on health gained from employment. Previously, employment was considered to have a negative influence on those with mental illness, and staff members often advised those clients who complained of subjective tiredness to cease working. Now, when the tool is used with family or staff members, they respect the client's choice and come to support his or her decisions.

The other main purpose of the intervention was to enable choice. This involved using a magnetic board to enable users to choose - with each client working as he or she prefers. In one sheltered workplace, the clients, with the author's assistance, created a monthly schedule on a magnetic board which listed the names of all the clients using the workplace. Clients wanting to commit to working in an integrated environment chose work tasks and placed magnets representing their various workplaces on the board. Clients' indication of choices through the magnet board is an important tool in this project - symbolizing that this project is occupation-based and client-centered.

Table 1
Questions to facilitate meaningful designing based on occupational science

Are you satisfied with the work that you chose?
Did you make a choice for meaningful designing based on your needs?
Does your chosen method of working match your subjective progress stage?
Describe your experience.
Are there sufficient choices for you to conduct meaningful designing?
Are you not overly tiring? What kind of strategies do you use?
How do you restore your mental and physical energy used at work?
How do you preserve your mental and physical energy to stay healthy?

Signs of movement toward an inclusive community

Through this practice, various job opportunities in the general environment were created, and clients each selected and developed their work meaningfully to start to work in the general environment. Because approximately 20 clients who use sheltered workshops succeeded in beginning to work in the community, staff at the sheltered workshops realised clients' employment potential and began to support all the clients who wanted to work. Those employed by, for instance, a social welfare council, a university, a cleaning company, or a city hospital received improved remunerations. Additionally, there is greater availability in the choices of job tasks such as office assistance, research assistance, reception, data input, printing, cleaning, and trash recycling. The number of those working with clients in integrated workplaces has increased, and the staff and families have come to respect clients' self-determination. At least one of the job partners has offered more work; furthermore, he proposed simplifications for the process. Finally, the city responded to a request to the mayor from clients for transportation by supporting public travel expenses for clients working in integrated workplaces. This was because the mayor understood that clients with mental illness can maintain healthy lives through working in the community and the cost of their transportation may be more than their remuneration where working hours are short.

These facts indicate that inclusion is being promoted simply through the occupation-based practice of aligning clients' needs with employment opportunities in the general workplaces.

Further challenges toward inclusion

Each experience was talked about by clients as follows:

'I have worked more than five years in the general workplace in the community. Year after year, my purpose in life - to be working with a sense of responsibility for the work - is stronger.'

'I came to the workshop last year. I'm not just at the workshop to be able to work in the general workplace, I am leading a full life.'

'Through working in the general workplace, I can learn how much I can work, how much I can step up, and how to make the best use of my physical energy.'

'When I started to work in the general workplace, I had to avoid hard work. But now, I can work to input the data using the office computer and printing. I appreciate having had the opportunity to work in the general workplace. This experience will be useful for my future.'

'Year after year, the company has entrusted me with increased work. So I have come to have increased self-confidence.'

The project has offered clients the opportunities to experience satisfaction from their contributions. Clients have enriched opportunities to experience different job choices through a network of employment support. The following strategy is required to realise the full potential of meaningful work. Through sharing information between network members regarding the choices required by clients for meaningful work, the project implemented a support network. Now, the project tries to share information with all network members. For instance, information on the Model and the clients' needs for working meaningfully must be shared among network members. Currently, the project requires leadership for an action plan to realise inclusive community through meaningful work.

In Japan, while the priority of employment support for people with mental illness has traditionally been focused on training and preparation, the availability of employment opportunities for those with mental illness has sharply decreased. When employment opportunities in general environments decreased, those with mental illness were unable to increase their experience through working and consequently acquire opportunities to promote meaningful work. On January 20, 2014, the Japanese government ratified the 'Convention on the Rights of Persons with Disabilities of the United Nations,' which urges the social participation of people with disabilities and bans discrimination against them. Subsequently, from April 2016, the legal mandating of related matters of reasonable accommodation will be enforced in Japan.

Reasonable accommodation does not mean creating *alternatives* to mainstream employment but supporting the participation of people with disabilities by implementing adjustments that create alternatives *within* the mainstream, one of the purposes of this project. As the legal mandating of matters related to reasonable accommodation will be enforced, we will need to emphasize *within* the mainstream in situations where exclusion policies continue, through promoting the realisation that people with mental disabilities can perform meaningful work, thus promoting inclusion. Further, we can focus on supporting designing with reasonable accommodation based on the Meaningful Work Design Model. We have recently begun the practice in a different community that creates alternatives to help people with mental illness enter the mainstream. In addition, we promulgate the realisation that people with mental disabilities can work in a manner similar to others but under different conditions created by the support network. Aichi Medical College is collaborating with Owari-Chubu Employment and Assisted Living Center for People with Disabilities in Aichi prefecture to create choices for people with mental disabilities who need to work in the community and to support mainstream employment for all clients.

In Japan, the Work Sharing Projects - in two different places, with different conditions - will continue to explore occupation-based practice and research, focusing on how to build occupationally inclusive communities.

References

Becker, D.R. and Drake, R.E. (2004) *A Working Life For People With Severe Mental Illness*. (Iwao Oshima translation supervisor). Tokyo, Japan: Kongo (pp.234-237)

Eklund, M., Hermansson, A. and Hakansson, C. (2012) Meaning in life for people with schizophrenia: Does it include occupation? *Journal of Occupational Science*, 19, 2,

Haertl, K. and Minato, M. (2006) Daily occupations of persons with mental illness: Themes from Japan and America. *Occupational Therapy in Mental Health*, 22, 1, 19-32

Leufstadius, C., Erlandsson, L.K., Björkman, T. and Eklund, M. (2008) Meaningfulness in daily occupations among individuals with persistent mental illness. *Journal of Occupational Science*, 15, 1, 27-35

Minato, M. and Zemke, R. (2004) Occupational choices of persons with schizophrenia living in the community. *Journal of Occupational Science*, 11, 31-39

Minato, M. (2009) Work sharing support working in a university–proposal and practice as occupational therapist to support 'I want to work', *Journal of Occupational Therapy*, Special issue, 43, 7, 646-648

Minato, M. (2010) How does work promote health, *Occupational Science Research*, 4, 1, 2-9

Minato, M., Yabuwaki, K., Iwata, M., Mimura, H., Nonaka, T. and Hashimoto, K. (2013) Kibi International University Work Sharing Project, *Kibi International University of Health and Welfare Research Institute Bulletin*, 14, 27-32.

Minato, M. (2014) Creating community to affirm all of the 'I want to work.' - Exploration and practice of the conceptual framework based on occupational science. in A. Tajima (Ed.), *'Affirming the existence' look to the occupational therapy.* Tokyo, Japan: Miwa (pp.64-81)

Minato, M., Horibe, Y. and Sakai, H. (2016) Work Sharing Project for inclusive employment support, *Aichi Medical College Bulletin.*

Ministry of Health Labor and Welfare (2013) *The Present Condition And The Subject Of Employment For People With A Handicap.* Ministry of Health Labor and Welfare [Accessed 10 September 2016 at http://www.mhlw.go.jp/file/05-Shingikai-11601000-Shokugyouanteikyoku-Soumuka/0000024508.pdf]

Ministry of Health Labor and Welfare (2015) *Job Assistance For People With Disabilities* [Accessed 10 September 2016 at http://www.mhlw.go.jp/file/05-Shingikai-12601000-Seisakutoukatsukan-Sanjikanshitsu_Shakaihoshoutantou/0000091254.pdf]

Rudman, D.L., Yu, B., Scott, E. and Pajouhandeh, P. (2000) Exploration of the perspectives of persons with schizophrenia regarding quality of life, *American Journal of Occupational Therapy*, 54, 137-147

Townsend, E. (1997) Occupation: Potential for personal and social transformation, *Journal of Occupational Science*, 4, 18-26

Villotti, P., Corbière, M., Zaniboni, S. and Fraccaroli, F. (2012) Individual and environmental factors related to job satisfaction in people with severe mental illness employed in social enterprises, *Work*, 43, 1, 33-41

World Federation of Occupational Therapists (2006) *Position Statement On Human Rights CM2006.* [Accessed 20 May 2016 at http://www.wfot.org/ResourceCentre.aspx]

Zemke, R. & Clark, F. (Eds.) (1996) *Occupational Science: The evolving discipline.* Philadelphia: F.A. Davis

Chapter 10
Shelter and food are not enough!
A Project for formerly homeless people in Austria

Susanne Mulzheim, Brigitta Hemmelmeier-Händel

The initial situation

Sophia (a pseudonym) is 34 years old. For five years she has been living in a studio in an apartment block: one bed-sitting room including basic kitchen facilities and a bathroom. It is her first flat and has been provided by the Viennese Assistance Programme for Homeless People. Sophia used to be homeless.

Sophia´s mother was a heavy drinker. When Sophia was four years old, she was taken from her mother and was raised in children´s homes until she was ten. Then she returned to stay with her mother. However, Sophia, then aged 16, and her mother were evicted, so she lived in different homes. Between 26 and 28 Sophia was homeless.

Sophia is not doing very well. She suffers from liver cirrhosis and hepatitis caused by her chronic heavy drinking. Additionally, she has problems in concentration, lacks drive and motivation, and lately she has been crying a lot. She increasingly withdraws from social contacts including the other people living in the house. Only her friend Esther comes to visit her daily. They consume alcohol together and watch TV.

Sophia is seen by an occupational therapist once a week. The occupational therapist previously created several raised beds for plants on the building´s roof. Now, together they tend the beds. It was Sophia´s wish to care for the plants. She says, 'This is the best day of the week. I do something useful. Without me the plants would not survive the heat on the roof.' During the rest of the week Sophia has no meaningful activity, which she experiences as very unsatisfactory. Sophia´s perception is supported by a study by Yanos et al. (2007). In the qualitative part of the study formerly homeless people were asked about their locus of meaningful activity. Of the sample, 38% stated that they do not engage in any meaningful activities; 'I lay in my bed and look at the walls' was an answer given by one of the participants.

The *Fonds Soziales Wien* is the provider of the Viennese Assistance Programme for Homeless People. This is a municipal provider of the city of Vienna with diverse social functions. One assignment is the Programme for Homeless People which maintains outpatient support and night shelters, a housing first programme[1], permanent housing and transitional accommodations, i.e. a total of 90 service settings in Vienna. These services are managed by sub-providers. The apartment block where Sophia lives is managed by a charitable association and includes 180 permanent apartments for formerly homeless people. If required, social workers support the residents at the apartment block with administrative procedures or financial questions. The residents have to be stabilized in their financial and health situation to obtain a flat and they have to pay a small rent. The garden around the building may be used by all residents.

Currently the garden is not used for any specific purpose. The results of a small survey completed by the social workers showed that some residents would like to create vegetable beds, while others would prefer a space to do crafts or to barbecue. At the moment this open space is only used by the male residents. It is the only *public* place in the apartment block where the men meet in groups and often get drunk. When women join them or have to pass by, the men are often rude. In order to avoid this unpleasant experience, most of the women do not use the space. Many of them have had prior experience with aggressive behaviour on the streets. They are traumatised by violence and therefore avoid the garden.

Nevertheless, there is another reason why the green space around the building is not being developed: the neighbours. The accommodation facility is located in a quiet residential area. There are some single-family houses around the apartment block. Repeatedly there have been understandable complaints about noise, pollution and fears about the residents setting bad role models for children. The charitable association, as the owner of the apartment block, wants to avoid further annoyance and consequently is very sceptical about an increased use of the open space.

The apartment block seems to be an inclusive opportunity for the community of formerly homeless people. It is an ordinary suburban building which allows the residents to live independently with acceptable habitable standards. Furthermore, the residents receive individual and financial support. Despite all this, the building is segregated. The people living there have no recognition and no stake in the community. They are excluded from society due to unemployment, substance abuse and financial hardship, and so many residents experience inequality in the community and denial by the neighbours.

The current assignment of the provider Fonds Soziales Wien, is to be responsible for the basic needs of homeless people (Fonds Soziales Wien, 2011), which includes housing and food. It does not implicate initiatives to promote social inclusion. Contrary to that we hold the view that shelter and food are not enough. `We´ are an occupational therapist and an open space planner. My specialisation as an occupational therapist is health promotion. An important experience during the development of several health promotion projects was that participation of the involved people in all project development steps is a critical success factor. My co-author works as an open space planner, also in charitable associations. She thus has practical experience in dealing with shelter providers and residents and knows how to make an open space available in cooperation with the users. Together we developed a vision for a participative project for formerly homeless people. However, the financial resources as well as the structural conditions are limited for offering new programmes.

The only way to establish a new (and different) programme is to start a funded project. In Austria a national fund promotes health promoting projects. The result of our talks with the representatives of the fund is a preliminary agreement to provide financial support on condition that the provider bears any additional costs. Usually the national fund covers two-thirds of the costs. However, the Fonds Soziales Wien and the charitable association are still reluctant for reasons which will be explained in the following paragraphs. The next section will outline what we have already been able to do to reach our vision and which further steps are necessary to start such a project.

Starting a project to promote social inclusion

The first essential step was talking to the municipal provider. At the first discussion with the head of the provider we realized that the Fonds Soziales Wien would neither hinder nor promote a project for social inclusion. Their financial means are very limited, so their focus is on housing only. It was clearly stated that our project would not be funded. However, they gave us permission to get in touch with sub-providers to arouse interest.

A potential sub-provider was the above mentioned charitable association, whose head and social workers we contacted. Several discussions have been held with the staff; the head never could attend. At the beginning the social workers were very sceptical. However, during the discussions the social workers developed an understanding of our vision. Unfortunately, we have not been able to reach an agreement yet, as soon after the deliberations all services for homeless people found themselves in a very difficult situation. The Austrian government decided to grant asylum to Syrian refugees, and such social services were involved. Many new hostels for asylum seekers had to be created, which resulted in understandable reservations to initiate new projects for homeless people. As a result the project parameters were not decided upon and the project planning was delayed.

Nevertheless, we would like to describe the steps of participative project development that we are planning to use to guide our work. For that purpose the Participatory Quality Development approach (Research Group Public Health et al., 2008) will be used, which particularly supports health promotion service providers in planning their work in collaboration with relevant stakeholders. This approach has been chosen because we are convinced that participation is a foundation to implementation of a project with its focus on social inclusion. Evidence from public health science shows intervention to be more effective and sustainable when the target group´s participation is increased (Rosenbrock, 2010).

In the context of the Participatory Quality Development approach participation means the chance to independently make decisions in essential areas of one´s own life: `The more influence people exercise in a decision-making process, the stronger is their participation´ (Research Group Public Health et al., 2008, n.p.). In order to describe the participative process better, the Research Group Public Health et al., (2008) developed a staged model. The different levels of participation are visualised in Figure 1.

Levels of Participation

community-owned initiatives	Goes beyond participation
decision-making authority	
partial delegation of decision-making authority	participation
shared decision making	
inclusion	
consultation	pre-stage of participation
information	
instruction	non-participatory level
instrumentalisation	

Figure 1: Levels of Participation (Research Group Public Health et al., 2008)

Please note that the term participation in this model does not relate to social participation or inclusion but to decision making. Hence, also the way the term inclusion is used in the model conveys a different meaning. Inclusion is a pre-stage of participation. The Research Group Public Health et al. (2008, n.p.) defines inclusion in a decision-making process as follows: `The service organisation asks selected members of the target group for advice (...). The advice received, however, is not guaranteed to influence decision-making´. This definition of *inclusion* differs from the definition of *social inclusion* which can be found in the next section.

The first step in a participative planning process is to convince participants to plan and implement the project together. The basic principle for a successful project is the cooperative collaboration of the people concerned (residents, neighbours, social workers, head of the charitable association) and the reflective analysis of who should be involved in decision-making processes and to what extent (Wright et al., 2010). This discussion is necessary as the same Level of Participation for all participants is neither possible nor useful. Realisation of participation depends on the life conditions of the community and the general set-up of the project (Research Group Public Health et al., 2008). With regard to our proposed project we analysed the current conditions for decision-making processes in the apartment block, which is illustrated in the first column in Figure 2. The second column presents the desired conditions.

Levels of Participation	Current condition	Desired condition
decision-making authority	head of the charitable association	head of the charitable association
partial decision-making authority	social workers	social workers
shared decision making		residents' spokespersons
inclusion	residents' spokespersons	residents, neighbours
consultation		
information	residents	
not involved	neighbours	

Figure 2: Possibilities for stakeholder participation

In the *current condition* problems of the residents as well as possible solutions are defined by professionals. The residents are usually only informed but not actively involved in decision making. Only if someone is interested in a special topic, are residents asked about their experiences. They have, however, only little knowledge about whether their ideas will be taken into consideration. The residents have elected spokespersons who are at the moment at the participation level of `inclusion´. They are asked for advice but there is no guarantee that it will be considered. Even though neighbours currently represent a significant barrier for the implementation of new programmes, they are not involved.

For successful participative project development it is necessary to build partnerships with representatives of the community and other relevant stakeholders. This necessitates critically reflecting on the possibilities of all concerned people to participate.

Head of the charitable association

The head of the charitable association has the decision-making authority. Therefore it has to be ensured that he accepts a participatory approach. In a briefing we intend to provide information about our suggestions. It is important to discuss any reservations and the legal responsibilities and to create a common picture of the goal. This can be supported by international examples of good practice. In a next step a meeting together with the head and the staff can be used to reflect on the benefit for all people involved and to discuss the existing hierarchies and their influence on participation. The traditional roles within a caretaker setting have to be considered and current roles have to be redefined in a useful way for the planned project. Changing the roles is an on-going learning process during the whole project progression. If the group agrees to start the project, a written agreement can be formulated.

Social workers

The social workers have been working with the residents for many years and have developed great expert knowledge. In their daily work with the residents the social workers experience difficulties. Most of the residents stay in their homes all day long and live very isolated lives. The social workers do not enter their homes except when they are invited, so it is hard to come in contact with the community. The social workers have reservations whether the residents would be interested in such a project. The residents have told the social workers that they want to be left in peace. In our discussion with the social workers we emphasized their resources such as their comprehensive experience. This expert knowledge is the foundation for the participative planning process and will be combined with the knowledge of other stakeholders as well as references. It has been stated that `Participatory Quality Development depends significantly on the local knowledge of stakeholders and assists them in utilising it, reflecting on and expanding this knowledge´ (Research Group Public Health et al., 2008, n.p.).

Residents' spokespersons

In our view it is essential to raise the level of participation for the spokespeople to the level of shared decision making. We have to realize that in a participative project it is a most difficult step to convince the representatives of the community to contribute. This step can last weeks to months (Research Group Public Health et al., 2008). In our case it is a great advantage that spokespeople are already available. The existing contact with the spokespeople can be used to attract additional residents who want to be involved in the project development. With a sufficient number of participants the wide range of needs and interests of the residents will be represented better. Yet, there are a number of probable obstacles which can hinder the development of this important partnership. Fisher and Hotchkiss (2008) stated that marginalized people, such as residents of homeless shelters, are vulnerable to developing a learned helplessness syndrome. As a consequence they feel they are unable to control their lives and destinies. Silver and Felix (1999) discussed executive function problems within the homeless population. These problems can be described as a lack of initiation, problems in setting goals, planning actions and evaluating the results of actions (Silver and Felix, 1999 in Raphael-Greenfield, 2012). The Research Group Public Health et al. (2008) stated that suspicion may hinder the collaboration and Torrey et al. (2005, in Ammeraal et al., 2013) noted that a lack of skills, knowledge and hope in the group of vulnerable people make it difficult to enter and continue an inclusion process. Also, in our practical work it becomes apparent that occurring symptoms of mental illness and substance abuse might be a barrier for participating. All these obstacles have to be discussed together in order to find strategies for collaboration.

Residents

The situation of the other residents is similar. Participants probably do not have the competencies or interest to make decisions. In the case of Sophia it is necessary to first strengthen her self-confidence or to arouse the wish to participate in essential decisions. She has not learned to formulate wishes or advocate her interests and consequently she needs a secure frame in order to participate. Initially a one-to-one conversation could be helpful for her. Her social connections need to be extended in order to strengthen her trust in others. Nevertheless, the residents´ level of participation should be extended from mere information to the level of inclusion. We have to develop suitable strategies to visualise the residents´ concerns, to include their needs and wishes in project development. The knowledge, insight and experience of the community are requirements to address real-world challenges (Raphael-Greenfield et al., 2015).

Neighbours:

In order to reduce the neighbours´ reservations, they need to be included. Due to the small number of neighbours around the residential home, personal conversations seem to be the most promising means of contact. The neighbours could be invited to discussions. Their common reservations are likely to enhance their interest in collaboration. Thus, the neighbours get an opportunity to voice their concerns and wishes and can contribute to finding solutions. The neighbours are important stakeholders who have to be involved. Otherwise the apartment block and the garden around it will not be an inclusive place for the residents because they are not welcome.

Projects focused on social inclusion are processes of change. To gain collaboration critical elements such as limited skills, suspicion and resistance have to be considered in all activities. Participants should have the certainty that their intentions will be included. The community has to understand that their dedication is the premise to reach their desired goals. The partnerships that are formed are prerequisites for the progress of the project.

In this developmental process all participants have the opportunity to learn and grow by working together. This does also applies to us as facilitators of this project. Our strengths are our knowledge in project development and strategic planning as well as our experiences with participative processes with socially disadvantaged people. However, it is a great challenge to develop such a project which incorporates our limitations as well. For example, we have had rare face-to-face contact with the residents and therefore have difficulties to assess their skills, limitations and suspicions. The social workers' expert knowledge, as well as the direct contact with the residents, is necessary to support our development and learning. The next paragraph outlines how we can learn more about and with the community with the help of participatory data collection methods.

Learning through the community

We have the vision that the project developed should increase social inclusion on a long-term basis. Ammeraal et al. (2013) understand social inclusion as a complex process that includes objective conditions and subjective experiences. Objective requirements of inclusive communities are, for example, facilities, legislation or funding. The subjective experience of inclusion depends on components such as `safety, trust in others, having the opportunity to grow or to be yourself´ (Ammeraal et al., 2013, p. 68). Many of the facts we know already show that there is a requirement for social inclusion.

We also believe in our hypothesis that the garden offers a good starting situation to address the residents´ needs and challenges for a number of reasons:

* The garden is located within the apartment block and can be created as a neighbourhood garden. There are 180 residents in the block and quite a number of these people indicated an interest in using the garden. The garden borders on other properties and thus offers a useful possibility to come in contact with the local community. Whatley et al. (2015) found that a supported community garden for people recovering from mental ill-health can create a sense of community for participants and local community members.
* The garden and its produce can be seen as an opportunity for meaningful occupations. The residents have only limited possibilities for occupations and experience little meaning in their lives. The offer of occupations in their natural environment enables people to find new roles and routines (York and Wiseman, 2012). Through meaningful occupations people feel less like outsiders and they contribute to society (Hvalsøe & Josephsson, 2003).
* With the garden a little piece of everyday life comes to the residents. The garden can increase the `feeling like home´ and the sense of belonging. We have realised that residents feel only slightly connected and do not feel at home in their appartments. Chan et al. (2014) stated that the extent of feeling like home correlates to community integration. Diamant and Waterhouse (2010, p. 84) confirmed that `a sense of belonging is a key element in enabling social inclusion through meaningful occupations´. Working collaboratively in the garden can be a positive anchor supporting the feeling of being rooted.
* My experience as an occupational therapist has shown that working with nature and the opportunity of various occupations are often described as motivating by the clients. Many describe flow experiences. This positively supports the (re-) acquisition of skills (Fieldhouse, 2003). Positive effects of gardening include, for example, improvement of togetherness, stronger feelings of social interaction

and inclusion (Sempik et al., 2014), increased level of independence, development of new abilities and skills and spiritual connection with nature (Fieldhouse & Sempik, 2007; York & Wiseman, 2012).

• By working together in the garden the residents can come in contact with others in a natural way. They can support and learn from each other and share the rough and the smooth. The garden is a public place where the residents can revel and accordingly strengthen social connections with other residents but also with the neighbours. So the garden can grow to be a safe place for all users.

But we have to be aware that this is our vision and our hypothesis. Sometimes it is necessary to develop a specific project plan in a small group at a given time when the partners are not involved yet, for example when you need a draft to negotiate terms with the provider. However, it has to be kept in mind that this is a preliminary plan which will be adapted and revised. Participative project planning means to plan with the people and not for the people (Research Group Public Health, 2008). We have to ensure that our ideas are flexible enough to incorporate the wishes and ideas of the partners.

Actually, we know little about the wishes and needs of the community. We have received some information about the residents from the social workers. Also, we have learned some things about Sophia. Additionally, we can obtain information from relevant literature. Thus, literature confirms that formerly homeless people often are not well integrated in society as a result of their restricted roles (Nemiroff et al., 2011; Speirs et al., 2013; Krabbenborg et al., 2013). Raphael-Greenfield et al. (2015) conducted in-depth interviews with formerly homeless people. From the results we want to highlight the category `constant fear and vigilance´. The participants in the study expressed fears of imprisonment, dying, assault, returning to using drugs, neighbourhood, losing their house and their future. One participant stated that his fears led him to an isolated existence and that he pursues many solitary occupations. He does not allow anyone into his home. All this information from a variety of sources will be combined and contributes to implicit perceptions of the community and the circumstances of how they live.

Derived from this evidence we can develop first assumptions about the needs of the community. Nevertheless, it is important to hear what the participants are saying. Therefore, we have to explore the needs, wishes and ideas of and with the participants. Because the garden seems to be a useful resource, we would suggest combining a needs assessment with the *using affordances*[2] of the garden. For that purpose it is necessary to collect information from all people involved. In the relevant literature you can find a great repertoire of participatory methods to collect data in communities, especially with disadvantaged social groups. Interactive methods help make participants partners and give insight to lived experiences which are often hidden in stories, narratives, jokes or visions (Wihofszky, 2013). This insight can be given mainly verbally, i.e. with rapid assessment, but also with a visual focus by using the photovoice method or community mapping. These methods can be adapted to the participant´s requirements or used in a mixed way. All three methods seem to be conducive to gaining a comprehensive picture of what the needs and wishes of the residents are and, on the other hand, of how the residents want to use the garden.

In rapid assessments short, topic-specific data are collected either orally or in written form for about 10 minutes (Research Group Public Health, 2008). Due to the brevity and the short concentration span of some of the residents this method appears to be appropriate for our community. We have to plan how to initiate conversations with the residents and the neighbours. The dialogue can be undertaken by the social workers. Alternatively, we can employ so-called ‘Multiplikatoren’. This is the Austrian term for community members who are trained to fulfil specific tasks in a project. Their closeness to the other members of the community often leads to more success. They get remuneration for their involvement, for example vouchers for grocery.

Alternatively, we could use the photovoice method. Members of the community take photos from their circumstances of life and tell each other the stories that led to the photos. So they can get a clearer picture of the community conditions and can reflect on the needs for change. The photovoice technique has already been used with homeless people (Community Tool Box, 2015).

Also community mapping can be used to combine needs assessment with using affordances. With this method the residents create maps which show the places where they stay generally and where the main places of their life are. They can also outline which places are used for which purpose. The results have to be discussed with the residents to determine the needs with respect to the different places.

All these methods are useful to get a clearer picture about the wishes and needs of all people involved and to learn from each other. The results will give us a direction where to go with the project.

Prospects

Since we have not completed the steps of developing partnerships and clarifying the community's needs, we can only hypothesise what might come next. We would like to develop our project into a neighbourhood garden. There are some good practice examples, such as ‘Sprout’ - a supported community garden in Melbourne. The results of an ethnographic study showed how community gardening at Sprout enabled social inclusion for people recovering from mental ill-health (Whatley et al., 2015). Sprout created a sense of community by establishing opportunities of working together in a welcoming and accepting culture. The participants were encouraged by support workers and volunteers in meaningful everyday activities in the garden, in the kitchen or at creative groups.

We could develop a plan for a neighbourhood garden using Sprout as a model. The social workers could attend as support workers and the neighbours could be involved as volunteers. We could identify activities which can be performed by the residents and adapt the garden for that purpose. But what will happen if we do so? We do not know if the residents, the social workers, and the neighbours would like this idea. We do not know if a neighbourhood garden is suitable to meet the residents' needs. And we have to bear in mind the difficulties and realities within this vulnerable community. Maybe the experiences of Sprout do not fit our community.

It is essential to realise that persistence on an idea might jeopardise the success of the whole project. When we conducted the first steps for the project we learned a lot about the importance of partnerships to promote social inclusion. We understand that partnerships are the foundation to create an atmosphere where learning and growing can occur. A prerequisite for that is, however, a change in perspective and attitude of all the people involved, which may be a great challenge in the existing system.

Notes

1. Housing First is an approach developed in the U.S., in which homeless persons are given access to accommodation of their own and, if needed, provided with mobile support in their homes´ (Fonds Soziales Wien, 2013, p.1). In this evidence-based strategy the consumer choice is a key component. The model is based on the wish of consumers who preferred `to have their basic needs met first by obtaining housing and then agreeing to obtain treatment´ (Raphael-Greenfield, 2012, p.137).
2. Using affordances is a technical term from landscape planning. It is a participative planning method that facilitates shared decision making by gathering information about intended usage of the available space.

References

Ammeraal, M., Kantartzis S., Burger, M., Bogeas, T., van der Molen, C. and Vercruysse, L. (2013) ELSiTO. A collaborative european initiative to foster social inclusion with persons experiencing mental illness. *Occupational Therapy International*, 20, 65-74

Chan, D.V., Helfrich, C.A., Hursh, N.C., Sally R.E. and Gopal, S. (2014) Measuring community integration using Geographic Information Systems (GIS) and participatory mapping for people who were once homeless. *Health & Place*, 27, 92-101.

Community Toolbox (2015) *Section20. Implementing Photovoice in Your Community*. [Accessed 28 Jan 2016 at http://ctb.ku.edu/en/table-of-contents/assessment/assessing-community-needs-and-resources/photovoice/main]

Diamant, E. and Waterhouse, A. (2010) Gardening and belonging: Reflections on how social and therapeutic horticulture may facilitate health, wellbeing and inclusion. *British Journal of Occupational Therapy*, 73, 2, 84–88

Fieldhouse, J. (2003) The impact of an allotment group on mental health clients´ health, wellbeing and social networking. *The British Journal of Occupational Therapy*, 66, 7, 286–296

Fieldhouse, J. and Sempik, J. (2007) Gardening without borders: Reflections on the results of a survey of practitioners of an 'unstructured' profession. *British Journal of Occupational Therapy*, 70, 10, 449–453

Fisher, G. and Hotchkiss, A. (2008) A model of occupational empowerment for marginalized populations in community environments. *Occupational Therapy In Health Care*, 22, 1, 55-71

Fonds Soziales Wien (2011) Obdachlos in Wien. [Accessed January 11, 2016 at http://wohnen.fsw.at/wohnungslos/]

Fonds Soziales Wien (2013) Abstract Housing First – The Viennese Model. [Accessed January 22, 2016 at http://wohnen.fsw.at/wohnungslos/]

Hvalsøe, B. and Josephsson, S. (2003) Characteristics of meaningful occupations from the perspective of mentally ill people. *Scandinavian Journal of Occupational Therapy*, 10, 2, 61–71

Krabbenborg, M., Boersma, S. and Wolf, J. (2013) A strengths based method for homeless youth: Effectiveness and fidelity of Houvast. *BMC Public Health*, 13, 359

Nemiroff, R., Aubry, T. and Klodawsky, F. (2011) From homelessness to community: psychological integration of women who have experienced homelessness. *Journal of Community Psychology*, 39, 8, 1003–1018

Raphael-Greenfield, E.I. (2012) Assessing executive and community functioning among homeless persons with substance use disorders using the executive function performance test. *Occupational Therapy International*, 19, 135-143

Raphael-Greenfield, E.I. and Gutman S.A. (2015) Understanding the lived experience of formerly homeless adults as they transition to supportive housing. *Occupational Therapy in Mental Health*, 31, 35-49

Research Group Public Health [Wright, M.T., Block, M., Unger, H.] and Deutsche AIDS-Hilfe (2008) Participatory Quality Development for Practice: an interactive internet resource for quality development for HIV prevention in aids service organizations. [Accessed 13 February 2015 at www.pq-hiv.de]

Rosenbrock, R. (2010) Vorwort: Partizipative Qualitätsentwicklung - um was es geht. in M.T. Wright (Ed.) *Partizipative Qualitätsentwicklung in der Gesundheitsförderung und Prävention*. Bern: Verlag Hans Huber, (9–12)

Sempik, J., Rickhuss, C. and Beeston, A. (2014) The effects of social and therapeutic horticulture on aspects of social behaviour. *British Journal of Occupational Therapy*, 77, 6, 313–319

Silver, J.M. and Felix A. (1999) Neuropsychiatry and the homeless. In F. Ovsiew (Ed.). *Neuropsychiatry and Mental Health Services*. Washington, DC: American Psychiatric Press, (319–333)

Speirs, V., Johnson, M. and Jirojwong, S. (2013) A systematic review of interventions for homeless women. *Journal of Clinical Nursing*, 22, 7-8, 1080–1093.

Torrey, W., Rapp, C., van Tosh, L., McNabb, C. and Ralph R. (2005) Recovery principles and evidence based practice: Essential ingredients of service improvement. *Community Mental Health Journal* 41, 91–100

Whatley, E., Fortune, T., and Williams, A. E. (2015) Enabling occupational participation and social inclusion for people recovering from mental ill-health through community gardening. *Australian Occupational Therapy Journal*, 62, 6, 428-437

Wihofszky, P. (2013) Die Praxis der Gesundheitsförderung zwischen Top-down und Bottom-up. Ansätze partizipativen Planens und Forschens in der Konzeptentwicklung. *Prävention und Gesundheitsförderung*, 8, 181-190

Wright, M.T. (Ed.) (2010) *Partizipative Qualitätsentwicklung in der Gesundheitsförderung und Prävention*. Bern: Verlag Hans Huber

Wright, M.T., Block, M. and Unger, H. (2010) Partizipation in der Zusammenarbeit zwischen Zielgruppe, Projekt und Geldgeber/in. in M.T. Wright (Ed.) *Partizipative Qualitätsentwicklung in der Gesundheitsförderung und Prävention*. Bern: Verlag Hans Huber, 75–91

Yanos, P.T., Felton, B.J., Tsemberis, S. and Frye, V.A. (2007) Exploring the role of housing type, neighborhood characteristics, and lifestyle factors in the community integration of formerly homeless persons diagnosed with mental illness. *Journal of Mental Health*, 16, 6, 703–717

York, M. and Wiseman, T. (2012) Gardening as an occupation: A critical review. *British Journal of Occupational Therapy*, 75, 2, 76–84

Chapter 11
Project Therapy, Education and Assimilation of Children with Handicap (TEACH):
A Community-based Rehabilitation Programme Template for Poor Communities

Abelardo Apollo I. David, Jr

Overview

15 million Filipinos live with some form of disability based on the United Nations' estimated global disability prevalence of about 15% (World Health Organization, 2015). The high cost of rehabilitation and related services, as well as the exodus of competent Filipino health workers and special education teachers for work overseas, make access to help even more difficult. In response to this predicament experienced especially in developing countries, the United Nations Convention on the Rights of Persons with Disabilities presents Community-based Rehabilitation (CBR) as a strategy that can promote the social inclusion of Persons with Disabilities (PWD) (International Labour Organization, United Nations Educational, Scientific and Cultural Organization, and World Health Organization, 2004). A central principle of CBR is empowering persons with disabilities and their families to help themselves. This is consistent with 'Nothing About Us, Without Us', a core advocacy of persons with disabilities in their struggle for self-reliance and integration. Variations of CBR have been implemented in the Philippines since the 1970's. However, it is widely acknowledged that many of these programmes struggle to thrive and to remain responsive to the people's needs (McGlade & Mendoza, 2009).

This chapter aims to present Project Therapy, Education and Assimilation of Children with Handicap (TEACH), an innovative CBR programme for children and youth with developmental conditions that effectively provides poor families access to a streamlined network of free medical, rehabilitation, wellness, educational and related services geared towards these youth and children's integration into society. The main processes entailed in setting up the programme and how the community participates will be detailed, with the hope of offering readers a framework for developing socially inclusive CBR programmes.

Through the years, Project TEACH has earned local and international recognition as a best practice in CBR. It is a joint project of the Rehabilitation and Empowerment of Adults and Children with Handicap (REACH) Foundation Inc., a non-profit organization founded by the author and Mandaluyong City. The city is one of the 16 cities that comprise Metro Manila, the National Capital Region of the Philippines. According to the 2015 census, it has a population of 386,276. It is the 14th most populous city in Metro Manila and the 6th smallest city in the Philippines with a land area of 11.06 km² (4.27 sq mi) (Wikipedia, 2021).

Setting-Up an Inclusive CBR Programme

Phase 1. Lay the Groundwork

Study the target community and organize the community.

A pioneer in setting up an office specifically for Disability Affairs, Mandaluyong City appealed as an ideal site for establishing a community-based rehabilitation programme. However, the city's positive reputation did not supersede the importance of objective information that would help ascertain the programme's relevance and sustainability. The city's poverty prevalence, the profile of people with disability and the resources available to them were among the parameters considered. Data gathered from the city's Persons with Disabilities Affairs Office revealed that a significant 25% of the people with disability consisted of individuals 18 years and below with developmental conditions and many of whom resided as informal settlers in *barangays or* villages densely populated by poor families. Earning a meager Php25,813/year (USD$530/year) (Philippine Statistics Authority, 2018), it was simply impossible for poorest families which comprise 16.7% of the population to provide for a child's much needed medical, therapy and educational services, informally estimated at USD$2940/year.

With the needs of children with disabilities confirmed, the REACH Foundation helped Mandaluyong City organize a forum among the stakeholders. Present in this forum were the City Mayor and other leaders from both the public and private sector. Appreciating how the CBR approach can foster health equity and social inclusion, the families of children with disabilities as well as local leaders expressed their willingness to participate in setting up a CBR programme from the ground. It was decided that Mandaluyong City would be a suitable site for a comprehensive CBR programme focusing on children.

Formalize partnerships

With the City Mayor being personally involved, the heads of pertinent local government offices such as the Department of Education, the Department of Social Welfare and Development, the Department of Health; Public Information Office; Persons with Disabilities Affairs Division; academia; church-based organizations; socio-civic and disability groups were invited to formally sanction the need for a CBR programme in the community. In 2007 a memorandum of agreement was signed by the above-mentioned stakeholders to define their roles and formalize their commitment to help establish a CBR project. This CBR programme was officially named Project Therapy, Education and Assimilation of Children with Handicap (TEACH), to reflect its ultimate goal of integrating differently abled children in mainstream society.

Develop programmes and service delivery protocols

Through collaborative consultations and workshops, a plan was drafted by the stakeholders with emphasis on the following elements: beneficiary eligibility criteria, problems to be addressed, programme objectives, general methodology, time-table, management team, community participation mechanism, sustainability mechanism and budget. The resulting service delivery protocol enabled grass root community helpers such as public school teachers, social workers, day care center workers, government hospital workers, *barangay* health workers, and civil society partners to locate and identify children who have or who were at risk of having developmental conditions. The poorest among these children were prioritized for the services. The succeeding sections detail how Project TEACH provides interventions for children.

Prepare space, materials and funding

Due to limited funds, therapy services were initially rendered in a small 60sqm room in a government community center. With the stakeholders, including family members contributing, the room was furnished with pre-loved furniture, toys and educational materials. More importantly, this helped foster *Bayanihan*, a Filipino custom which refers to the spirit of communal unity (Manila Bulletin, 2015).

Through the years, the impact that Project TEACH has made on the lives of more than 1,200 children and their families has created much good will and public awareness. Winning best practice citations and awards both locally and abroad, Project TEACH's track record has helped convince funding agencies and corporations such as the Australian Government and *Manulife*, a private multinational insurance firm, to provide support through grants. The most recent recognition Project TEACH has received was the 2015 United Nations Public Service Awards for Improving the Delivery of Public Services (United Nations Department of Economic and Social Affairs, 2015). The funds generated from both the government and the private sector ushered Project TEACH to its permanent home in a modern three-story building at the heart of a beautiful park that was once a dumpsite. For many families in this heavily populated urban poor community, this facility now serves as an oasis for hope and healing (Abalos, B., personal communication, October 14, 2015). Home visits are undertaken for children whose families cannot bring them to the site for therapy. This might be due to the absence of guardians who can supervise the child's other siblings if they are left at home. Other children have elderly or disabled guardians who find transporting the child to the site physically challenging. The absence of funds to pay for transportation fares is another common reason for this. Special education and medical services are conveniently provided in regular public schools and health centers, respectively. Project TEACH has ultimately achieved its goal of being fully sustained by the local government.

Recruit and empower human resources

Special education teachers, occupational, physical and speech therapists were recruited and trained on how to provide services following a community-based and client-centered rather than a medical and disability-focused approach. Here, therapists strongly consider the client's priorities and goals; families are taught how to carry out therapy procedures at home and interventions are contextualized according to the resources available in the community. Interns who train in the center significantly augment the manpower. In Project TEACH, the interns' performance is evaluated not just in terms of their handling skills but mainly by how well they teach parents to handle their children.

Since all services are offered for free, the parents of beneficiaries are encouraged to render community-services to deter a dole-out culture. Some parents volunteer as Community Rehabilitation and Education Workers (CREW) who assist the staff in implementing therapy and educational programmes after undergoing training. Other parents help in housekeeping by keeping the facilities clean and orderly. Some participate in awareness and advocacy drives for persons with disabilities.

Phase 2. Implement the Programme

Surveillance and eligibility screening

Through seminars and workshops, grass roots community helpers and volunteers were oriented to the key symptoms of various developmental conditions such as Autism, Intellectual Disability, Attention Deficit Hyperactivity Disorder, Dyslexia, Cerebral Palsy and Down Syndrome by the REACH Foundation, Inc. Equipped with this knowledge, they then went door-to-door in poor communities, to locate every child with disability. Residents whose children are suspected to have developmental delays are respectfully advised to bring their children to the nearest health center for proper screening and help.

Developmental assessment and diagnosis

Children referred to the health centers are screened by government doctors for developmental delays. Moreover, these doctors address presenting physiological issues. For instance, vitamins and medicines are given to malnourished and immuno-compromised children. If specialized diagnostic procedures are necessary, the children are referred to developmental pediatricians who come to Project TEACH regularly. These specialists administer appropriate tests to confirm or to rule out a diagnosis. If a diagnosis is confirmed, the doctor conducts family counseling and explains the implications of the diagnosis on the child's development. With the assurance that the city can offer the children necessary interventions for free, families find hope (Abalos, B., personal communication, October 14, 2015).

Offer Interventions

Project TEACH offers a comprehensive array of services and interventions which include medical and dental services, counselling, assistive technology, work placement, sports and recreational programmes. In this chapter, the discussion will focus on Project TEACH's innovative therapy, educational and vocational skills training programme.

Transfer of learning through interdisciplinary therapy and tutorial services
Occupational therapy, physical therapy, speech therapy and special education staff conduct an initial evaluation during their first meeting with the child. This is to identify the child's activity limitations and the internal and contextual factors that lead to these. Therapy and educational programmes that can be feasibly implemented in the child's natural home environment are then developed. The staff initially implements this programme alongside a CREW and the child's parents so as to demonstrate and explain the procedures. Eventually, the staff assumes a more supervisory role as the CREW begins to more actively facilitate the therapy and/or tutorial sessions. The CREW then transfers the knowledge and skills to the child's parents who are expected to carry out the instruction at home. To ensure a cohesive management, the therapists and teachers employ an interdisciplinary approach whereby they closely communicate to streamline their assessment procedures, goals and intervention strategies towards promoting the child's activity participation, role fulfilment and social inclusion.

Transdisciplinary home care therapy services.
Beneficiaries of Project TEACH who cannot travel to the center are given home-care services. Due to manpower and budgetary constraints, only one CREW and a staff or intern can visit a particular child's home. Since many of these children present with multiple disabilities, the staff and CREW employ a transdisciplinary approach (TDA). In the TDA, therapists function as generalists wherein they safely implement interventions learned from within their profession as well as basic procedures endorsed by colleagues from other disciplines (Magallona and Datangel, 2011). For instance, in helping a child with cerebral palsy to participate in a play activity in school, an occupational therapist may carry-out spasticity inhibition, speech and language stimulation and reading intervention techniques in consultation with a physical therapist, speech therapist and a special education teacher, respectively.

Standardized special, mainstreaming and inclusive education
Prior to Project TEACH, public school special education teachers were confronted with the challenge of managing large classes of students with varying medical, academic and behavioral profiles. It was determined that a main factor which led to such highly heterogeneous class composition was the absence of a body which screened the students and matched them to schools that offered the most suitable educational programmes for them. It was observed that previously, some students were assigned to a particular school and class based on uni-dimensional rationales. For instance, a teacher or therapist only considered the child's age or diagnosis in determining his or her class. Similarly, some parents choose a school based on proximity without consideration of the programme's appropriateness to their child's needs.

Through Project TEACH, an interdisciplinary team of professionals was organized and tasked to screen all children with disabilities enrolled in and who were about to enter the public school system, many of whom were five to six years old. This team organized the students into more homogenous groups taking into account factors such as their age, gender, diagnosis, interests, goals, developmental skills and behaviors. Although all public schools offer mixed classes, some are all boys largely due to the higher incidence of disability in males. Some parents of female students feel uncomfortable about their daughter being the only girl in a class, and ask for them to be taught with other female students. Other families prefer the teacher to be of a specific gender, usually when girls' parents ask for them to be taught by women. Moreover, Project TEACH has assigned 'specialty programmes' for Mandaluyong City's public schools as a practical solution to their limited funds, staffing and physical facilities. For instance, a school could focus on early education, functional academics or pre-vocational skills classes depending on its expertise and available resources. If necessary, free transportation services were offered to students who have been matched to schools that are farther to their residence.

Project TEACH endeavours to mainstream and include as many adequately trained students with special needs as possible in regular classes. Mainstreamed students enjoy the benefit of a modified curriculum that is appropriate to their learning capacity and needs. On the other hand, students in the inclusion programme can manage the regular academic curriculum intellectually but may have behavioural issues that would require some accommodations in terms of teaching strategies and classroom environments. For quality assurance, teaching and management protocols were standardized. Prior to integrating a child with special needs in a regular classroom, sensitivity training focusing on respect for individual differences is conducted for school heads, teachers, staff, parents and students. Tools such as the Diversity and Inclusion for Modules for Preschool to Late Elementary Students (DIMPLES) were developed to facilitate the creation of more supportive school ecosystems. The DIMPLES was created through a grant received from The Atlantic Fellows for Health Equity in Southeast Asia and the Australian Aid. A quasi-experimental research was conducted to determine the said modules' effectiveness on Filipino students. Results revealed that there is a statistically significant difference with 95% confidence interval in the overall diversity and inclusion competencies of participating typically developing students in the experimental group before and after the DIMPLES as perceived by their teachers.

Vocational skills training and employment
Vocational skills training is provided for adolescents and young adults to prepare them for future employment pursuits. Through 'Kitchen Specials' (KS), a social enterprise set-up within a public school, students are taught vocational skills such as food service and food preparation. KS supplies public school canteens with nutritious and affordable snacks. Part of the KS income is shared with the students to help augment their families' income. The Manpower and Youth Development Training Center of Mandaluyong City, a government agency mandated to teach technical and vocational skills, has also opened its diverse vocational programmes, such as carpentry, automotive repairs, beauty care and massage, to youth with disabilities. Ultimately, the Persons with Disabilities Affairs Division of the city is engaged to help adequately prepared people with disabilities find employment. Part of the work placement process entails job coaching the students and training business establishments on how to work most effectively with persons with disabilities.

Phase 3. Evaluate, Sustain and Replicate

All the stakeholders meet at least once a month to evaluate Project TEACH's programmes and to discuss ways to enhance these accordingly. Internal evaluation processes include measuring performance outcomes and client satisfaction. In the most recent quality assurance survey conducted by Project TEACH in 2019, 97% of the parent respondents observed improvements on their children, 100% felt that interventions given were appropriate and 100% of the parent respondents expressed satisfaction over the services rendered.

When the City Council of Mandaluyong institutionalized Project TEACH through a City Ordinance making it a permanent programme of the city, the dream became to inspire other individuals, organizations and/or local government units to establish similar CBR programmes in their respective communities. To demonstrate the replicability of the programme, other local governments have established their own CBR programme inspired by Project TEACH. Moreover, delegates from countries such as Canada, East Timor, India, Laos, Mongolia, The United Kingdom and Vietnam have come to learn about the Project TEACH CBR Model. Project TEACH aspires to help the Philippines graduate from being a recipient of technology to becoming an innovator that contributes new knowledge for the global advocacy of barrier-free society for persons with disabilities.

Project TEACH from various standpoints. Narratives on social transformation

Tanya, staff occupational therapist

As a staff occupational therapist, my main role is to train, assist and supervise the interns, CREW and parents. In training the CREW and parents, we refrain from using technical jargon. We communicate using their own language and we need to be sensitive to their culture so as to facilitate learning and mutual respect.

Together with CREW, we conduct home therapy services using materials that are available in the child's home. Often, we need to improvise and indigenize. For example, we make toys out of empty canisters and scrap materials. This is very different to private clinics where therapists have access to all types of toys and therapy materials. Family education is key, for it allows the child to receive needed interventions even when we are not around. Among our goals is included facilitating independence in school, play and self-help activities. Compensatory as well as remedial interventions such as behavior modification, sensory integration and speech and language stimulation techniques are employed to help our students achieve optimum activity participation.

In other areas, one can only avail of therapy sessions from either hospitals or private centers. Normally, these facilities' charges are very high. The more affordable government centers would often subject clients to a long waiting list and may be too distant to their house. This programme, with its affordability and proximity is really beneficial to the community.

Our programme has been visited by other local and international organizations. Most recently, a University in Canada has formally sent interns to us to train in community-based rehabilitation. These are indicators that Project TEACH is being recognized as a good practice model.

Dicky, father of a child with autism

I am parent of a child with autism named Paulo. As parents, our primary role is to bring our children to the center for their therapy sessions in order to promote their development. We help out voluntarily to do some work such as house-keeping and cleaning of the facilities. I help by driving the center's utility vehicle to transport mobility-challenged children. Other parents, like my wife, volunteer to be trained to serve as a CREW. This way, they get to help other children like our son.

We assist in our child's therapy sessions. We give the staff, interns and CREW some insights on how we feel they can work better with our child. When I see a child with disability, I tell the parents of that child how they can avail of the same services my son is benefiting from.

As parents and CREW, we do our best to be active in advocacy groups such as the Autism Society Philippines (Autism Society Philippines, 2014). We have support groups available especially for parents who are still in denial. We tell them not to hide their children and that through programmes such as Project TEACH their children can still learn and develop.

Since services are free in Project TEACH, our family is able to save money for our most essential needs. In addition, Project TEACH has allowed us to partake in different sports, recreational and educational activities where we are able to interact with other parents and where our children can socialize. Many parents and CREW recognize that Project TEACH has helped develop among them an enhanced sense of purpose and community.

As parents, we have noticed that the people of our community are becoming more aware about the disability of our children. Differently-abled children can now socialize with typically developing children, unlike before where they are usually left alone and isolated.

In the beginning, Paulo would grab things impulsively. This has changed. In fact, he can now go to a local store to request and buy items. Due to community awareness campaigns, people such as our local storekeeper would not easily get angry whenever children with special needs would grab their wares. They are now more understanding. Sometimes, they would even give the children candy. It gives me so much joy seeing children in our neighborhood inviting my son to play with them. I distinctly remember an instance where there was a riot brewing in my neighborhood. The people on the street were vigilant and were one in telling Paolo 'Kuya (Kuya is a Filipino term of respect which means big brother) Paulo! Go home! Go home!' Seemingly simple gestures like this mean very much to us parents. Seeing this social transformation gives us much hope.

Melissa, CREW

Since we are not professionally trained health workers, we provide therapy to children under the guidance and supervision of staff and interns. The numerous seminars and workshops given to us have helped equip me and other CREW to work more effectively with children with special needs and their families.

Project TEACH has been a big help to the children. I have worked with children who were severely challenged. After receiving therapy, they have slowly learned important life skills. Seeing them being able to regulate their behaviors, move more easily, communicate and perform activities of daily living more independently gives us CREW an immense sense of fulfillment.

I envision that one day we would be capable of rendering more home care sessions, especially in the slums. There are many other children whose families cannot bring them to the center for valid reasons. For instance, some children only live with grandparents who are too frail to accompany them to the center. Other families barely have enough money to pay for their fare to the center.

Joker, physical therapy intern

As an intern, it is my responsibility to learn how to handle children with different conditions and to teach parents and CREW how to help these children develop their skills optimally. We prepare home programmes and personally demonstrate to the parents how to implement these at home. I sense a stronger sense of hope among parents in Mandaluyong City. I believe this is largely due to the fact that they are informed about their rights and are empowered to help their children.

Since I get to work closely around professionals from other disciplines, better awareness and appreciation about each other's role is attained. I have heard and learned about CBR in the school but it is very different when you are actually immersed in it. It is positively overwhelming to witness that programmes such as Project TEACH exist to help the poorest of the poor. I wish that Project TEACH can be replicated in other communities where the situation is dire for people with disabilities. Seeing the impact of my work as an intern on the children I work with and on their families boosts my confidence and this helps me become more passionate about my work.

Benjamin, Jr., Mandaluyong City Mayor

A couple of years ago, there was a media craze about a student with Autism who graduated at the top of his class in a private school. I remembered being so impressed and inspired by his story. That evening on my way home, I stumbled upon a street child who evidently showed signs of Autism such as hand flapping, while lying naked on the wet sidewalk pavement. The sight pulled my heart, almost bringing me to tears. I asked, 'Why could one child with Autism achieve so much yet another be in such despair?' It was because the first boy came from a loving family which had the means to extend to him all the support and interventions he needed to succeed. At that moment, I resolved that the city will empower itself to be a good mother to what turned out to be hundreds of children with special needs from poor families.

It was providential that I was introduced to Prof. David, the president of REACH Foundation, a young gentleman who happened to share my vision of enabling children with special needs to become independent, happy and integrated members of society. I knew that we would make a formidable team in establishing a CBR programme. Consolidating our resources, ideas and efforts with our partners', we were able to establish Project TEACH which since 2007, has touched the lives of more than 1200 children. Today, our city, through the tremendous impact that Project TEACH has made, has inspired colleagues from the government to take concrete and similar action. To quote Prof. David, 'What is disabling is not the condition of the child per se but the wrongful attitudes of those around him.' Our city commits to continue serving as a catalyst of national transformation for a more disability inclusive society.

Key Factors to Success

Project TEACH is a good example of how the private and public sector can work together. The sustainability of this collaboration was promoted by a Memorandum of Agreement which defined and formalized the roles, responsibilities and expectations of each stakeholder. More importantly, the community lobbied for legislation that institutionalized Project TEACH.

Project TEACH demonstrated that it is not merely about building state-of-art facilities. Instead, investments were focused on hiring and continuously developing the best and most service-oriented staff and CREW possible. In time, the programme's outcomes attracted more benefactors and better facilities were built.

The project underscores the value of community empowerment and transfer of knowledge. CREW members and volunteer parents underwent training to enable them to assist in the implementation of therapy and educational programmes. To prevent a dole-out culture, the parents of beneficiaries are encouraged to render community-services that suited their schedules, interests and skills. This cost-effective model can help strengthen communities that constantly face the threat of the exodus of qualified Filipino therapists and teachers for work abroad.

Proper documentation facilitated the objective of inspiring other local governments to replicate Project TEACH in their respective communities. Accomplishment reports submitted to partners projected transparency and a sense of collaboration.

A multi-sectoral approach facilitated the creation of a streamlined service delivery framework. This proved to be cost-effective since it allowed sharing of resources and it prevented work redundancy. Regular meetings attended by representatives of all the sectors concerned, allowed the programme to evolve accordingly and to stay responsive to the community's needs.

References

Abalos, B. (2015, October 14) Personal Interview

Autism Society Philippines (2014) *Autism Society Philippines.* [Accessed 24 January 2016 at http://www.autismsocietyphilippines.org/]

International Labour Organization, United Nations Educational, Scientific and Cultural Organization, and World Health Organization (2004) *CBR: A Strategy for Rehabilitation, Equalization of Opportunities, Poverty Reduction and Social Inclusion of People with Disabilities: Joint Position Paper.* World Health Organization [Accessed 19 January 2016 at http://apps.who.int/iris/bitstream/10665/43060/1/9241592389_eng.pdf]

Magallona, M.L. and Datangel, J. (2011) The community based rehabilitation programme of the University of the Philippines Manila, College of Allied Medical Professions. *Disability, CBR and Inclusive Development,* 22, 3, 36-61

Manila Bulletin (2015) *Information: Keeping alive the Filipinos' Bayanihan Spirit.* [Accessed 24 January 2016 at http://www.mb.com.ph/information-keeping-alive-the-filipinos-bayanihan-spirit/]

McGlade, B. and Mendoza, V.E. (2009) *Philippine CBR Manual: An Inclusive Development Strategy.* Philippines: CBM

Philippine Statistics Authority (2018) Poverty Press Releases

United Nations Department of Economic and Social Affairs (2015) *2015 United Nations Public Service Award Winners.* [Accessed 19 January 2016 at http://workspace.unpan.org/sites/Internet/Documents/Winners%20of%202015%20United%20Nations%20Public%20Service%20Awards.docx.pdf]

Wikipedia (2021) *Mandaluyong.* [Accessed 17 March 2021 at https://en.wikipedia.org/wiki/Mandaluyong]

World Health Organization (2015) *World Report on Disability.* [Accessed 1 October 2015 at http://www.who.int/disabilities/world_report/2011/report/en/]

Chapter 12
Community development through community support projects by occupational therapists

Hajime Morishima, Kazunari Daigo

The authors, Hajime and Kazunari, both believe that occupational therapists can support environmental coordination to match social needs. Therapists can do this by adjusting or giving advice on domestic equipment, making communal facilities more user-friendly, introducing public services or by providing consultation on better communication with persons with certain difficulties. Occupational therapists can work towards social participation for all, so that people can access more opportunities in their lives, regardless of their abilities or their household incomes.

Hajime has been involved in a *pro bono* group of nine occupational therapists who, in addition to voluntarily tackling social issues, all work at hospitals or teach at professional training colleges. This group was established in response to a call (described below) from Kazunari, with the aims of developing a social contribution to support elderly people in the community in enjoying longer healthy life expectancy, and to promote healthy development in children.

Kazunari has been active in social contribution and community activities for a long time. Until June 2015 he was an occupational therapist at the Medical Corporation Meiho-kai Shin Totsuka Hospital, Yokohama City, Kanagawa Prefecture, where he was in charge of rehabilitation for hospitalized patients as well as personnel management. Kazunari left and in August 2015 established the Laule'a (peace, happiness and friendship) non-profit organization. While visiting New Zealand under a program organized by the Cabinet Office of Japan (2013) to learn how persons with disabilities participate in social activities, he observed some person-centered activities based on the social model of disability. Kazunari (Daigo, 2015) found that many New Zealand occupational therapists are active in their communities. Through their community-based and social contribution activities occupational therapists have been recognized as essential workers for persons with disabilities.

In Japan occupational therapists provide their services under medical and long-term care insurance schemes. Their services are provided under the coverage of these insurances and only with medical doctors' prescriptions for occupational therapy. While it is possible to provide services outside these schemes, few occupational therapists do so as it is very difficult to set up and continue their businesses. About 70% of occupational therapists work at hospitals or care facilities and very few are active in community- based intervention.

Under these circumstances, Kazunari has explored ways for occupational therapists to organize community and social contribution activities in their leisure time besides working at hospitals or care facilities. One solution is *pro bono* activity, where therapists voluntarily use their professional skills to provide services for the public good, with three pillars of 1) establishing networks among occupational therapists and other professionals sharing similar visions; 2) organizing seminars to further enhance the skills of occupational therapists, and 3) implementing community and social activities, taking advantage of occupational therapists' professional skills.

At present, this *pro bono* group promotes the potential of occupational therapy interventions outside medical or care facilities and organizes workshops to improve occupational therapists' skills in order to create opportunities to practice the ten key enablement skills identified by Townsend (2009): adapt, advocate, coach, collaborate, consult, coordinate, design/build, educate, engage and specialize.

Besides this *pro bono* group, Hajime has established an approach to enable elderly people and youth to enjoy healthy living in their communities, including prevention of dementia symptoms and the raising of health awareness, by collaborating with municipal governments and various organizations upon requests for their community activities.

The purpose of voluntary activities by occupational therapists

Hajime believes that when organizing easy-to-join and ethically-based activities voluntary work offers the best basis for finding persons who can easily lend a helping hand to people in need and to organize activities, but funds are required to establish an activity or to take initiatives. In order to maintain activities and to include staff and experts a stable system of revenue from products and services is recommended as some participants may be resistant to being given charity. In Hajime's experience participants should pay a fee according to their circumstances.

In many cases, occupational therapists are expected to enrich the daily lives of the people with physical or mental disabilities whom they engage with and treat. However, any individual may recognize some kinds of difficulty in everyday life not only those with disabilities. Thus, potentially, everyone's activities could be the targets of occupational therapists' interventions. Hajime believes that occupational therapists may possibly contribute their expertise to the future of growing diversity by supporting every person to participate in various social activities regardless of differences in living, physical or mental conditions. Occupational therapy may offer society the means to become more inclusive, supporting diversity, an improvement that may benefit every individual. Activities concerning raising awareness for health amongst both young and older people through occupational therapy gave Hajime an opportunity to think deeply about social issues where occupational therapists could still intervene.

Occupational therapists are experts in making adaptations to the living environments of their clients. Through improving their clients' home environment and enabling them to use adaptations effectively it is expected that occupational therapists may also improve their clients' lives. But changes can also be made to the surrounding environment through the input of occupational therapists into providing public facilities, traffic signs and shop interiors with universal designs that are accessible for everyone. These changes might not be proposed by other professional groups. While living in Yokosuka, another city in Kanagawa Prefecture, Hajime used these perspectives with a project to utilize 'vacant houses' for the homeless, as described later in this chapter. Although his involvement in the project ended at the beginning of 2015, Hajime still believes in the effectiveness of this approach for the community and hopes to resume the projects by disseminating the impact generated by these initiatives to the municipal government and other organizations.

Hajime has organized another project, similar to that in Yokosuka, in Shitamachi, a downtown community in Tokyo where he now resides. Shitamachi has similar issues to Yokosuka, such as homeless people, elders living alone in their own homes isolated from society, children waiting for nursery school places (as parents have to work for their living but are unable to find a nursery school for their children because schools are already full), and children of families living in poverty. Hajime understands that occupational therapists are able to provide professional consultation for these issues and cooperate with non-profit organizations. Some examples of such organizations that are a support for homeless people are the non-profit corporation 'Tenohashi' (http://tenohasi.org/); bridging a gap between residents and medical organization in a community by Kurashi-no-hokenshitsu, a project organized by the Hakujuji (White Cross) Outreach Nursing Station (2016) (http://www.cares-hakujuji.com/services/kurashi); and the promotion of 'Housing First' projects by Médicins du Mundo (http://www.mdm.or.jp/). Hajime has worked to establish an organization to provide a 'third place' for citizens where various consultations are available as a one-stop service station for those who do not know where else to gain advice for their issues. He has invited the city government, local business enterprises and community cafés to contribute support either financially, through work, or the use of venues. As such, he believes that local residents could recognize occupational therapists not only as rehabilitation professionals but also for other various roles through their capacity to be community facilitators. Examples are given below.

Major voluntary activities to support others

Supporting homeless people through night patrols to survey their living needs.

One of the issues faced by several city governments in Kanagawa Prefecture is the number of homeless people, who often do not know how to apply for social security benefits and free medical examinations. Although municipalities have schemes to assist these people once their applications have been made, without access to health administration or social security it is difficult for them to go to hospital when they are in need of medical care. For over 20 years a spontaneous organization in Tokyo and Kanagawa Prefectures has been implementing night patrols which ask people about their health conditions, whether they have work and an income, or whether they are aware of the availability of social security. The organization (which has no name but has a website concerned with the working poor http://www.geocities.jp/kotobukisienshakouryuukai/contents.htm), works in collaboration with professional associations and various volunteer members, including occupational therapists, amongst them Hajime himself, as well as certified 'administrative procedures legal specialists' (registered specialists to facilitate administrative procedures on behalf of claimants), medical doctors, nurses, psychiatric social workers, day care staff of Alcoholics Anonymous recovery facilities, citizens and persons with disabilities. Many of the volunteers have professional connections with city governments or hospitals. The homeless people who are found in need of care or support during night patrols are introduced to the authorities or facilities with these connections. The organization sets the dates for night patrols with members' voluntary participation, but does not raise funds for their activities.

Yokosuka project to reuse vacant houses with ideas of occupational therapists: vacant houses are societal resources.

As the economy has developed over the 20th and 21st century, workers have drastically decreased their involvement in community activities and, as their living conditions have become much comfortable, they have put more value on their individual lives than on the community; therefore, individual ties or bonds with communities have become weaker (Yamaguchi, 2015). Post-World War II Japanese society has become more or less similar to many modern states in the world. In the *Edo* (1603-1878) or early *Showa* (1925-1945) era Japan used to have a social system that highly valued community ties and family bonds: mutual aid was organized among neighbors in groups of 5 or 10 members (called *Gonin-gumi* for 5 members or *Junin-gumi* for 10), while family traditions were inherited for generations. More recently, however, family units have become dispersed as people moved away from the country to the cities to look for work and establish new ways of life. However economic developments in Japan have also seen the break-up of traditional paternalistic working relationships between employers and their employees (at one time people were able to assume they would be employed until retirement and would receive a good pension) and the social welfare system has not been adequate to deal with the consequences (Kingston, 2011).

Generally in Japan families in poverty have been socially isolated in their communities without being able to solve their problems. They have faced difficulties in providing enough support or sufficient education for their children's development needs. Limited opportunities for additional education have left the children in poverty without improving their living conditions or enabling them to learn how to communicate with other people. Their stress tolerances have become lower, which may in turn predispose them for developmental or mental disabilities (Mugiwara, 2013; Sawamura, 2013; Sugawara, 1993). Therefore, community development to revive social and communal bonds between people is urgently needed for the residents to establish a system for mutual support.

In recent years some groups of sociologists, doctors, nurses and other professionals have established community cafes in towns; nurses have established healthcare rooms where people easily stop by for a medical check-up, such as blood examinations. Occupational therapists' involvement has also increased: one example is Minkuru cafe as described below. Hajime and Kazunari have invited other occupational therapists to join in such activities on a *probono* basis.

Hajime, whose involvement in the project ended at the beginning of 2015, worked with the mayor or city council members with the cooperation of the owners of vacant houses to locate various welfare services in them for the benefit of other community residents who live nearby. In some communities it is anticipated that vacant houses and rooms which are currently used for community gatherings will be needed by newcomers. However, in other communities there is an increase in the number of vacant houses or rooms which are not utilized. Vacant houses or rooms could be used in association with small multi-care facilities for elderly people. These Small Multi-care Facilities, such as 'Otagaisan' and 'Yurari-kan'[1], provide care for the elderly as well as support for their family members. In addition these facilities organize activities where the elders find their motivation in fulfilling all their roles. These facilities have established their own communities by organizing multigenerational interaction and looking after elders who live alone. The rooms can also be used to develop community activities with persons with mental health problems, child nursery centers, and have enabled the social participation of community residents and elderly people. There is a plan to utilize vacant houses for homeless people as shelters.

Project vision

The Yokosuka project aims for every person to be able to continue living in a familiar environment by receiving comprehensive support within the community whatever the difficulty. Its purpose is to use vacant houses and rooms to provide small multi-care facilities for elderly people and community activities for persons with mental disabilities or child nursery centers, applying an occupational therapy perspective. As people come and gather at these houses and rooms, it also aims to promote interaction and mutual support, for which it is necessary for community residents to recognize other residents who are socially isolated and provide support with their skills and time to those in need. The aim is to prevent any person being isolated or without social interaction. Through the project Hajime has organized workshops to enable community residents to interact through the renovation of vacant houses, barbecues and shared cooking. Ultimately, this approach may prevent people being left out of their communities, or isolated.

Utilizing vacant houses or rooms

Regularly scheduled tours to visit vacant houses with community residents enable participants to learn the history of the area and resources available in the community. The tours promote idea-sharing with residents or other participants about organizing activities to match community needs, so that full use can be made of the vacant houses. Public administrations have been collaborating to help organize this project: providing explanations during the tours, renewing a grant system, and giving support to obtain co-operation with mass media so that multi-care facilities can be established.

'Shitamachi' occupational therapist *pro bono* team 'OCCULABO, occupational lab' trying to get everyone downtown to be active!

The same concept has been applied in the *'Shitamachi'* or literally the 'low city' of Tokyo. Official figures for the population in the targeted areas at the time of writing (2016) were 193,156 in Taito City (Ward), 264,350 in Sumida City and 504,362 in Koto City.

In July 2015, Hajime established a volunteer group of professionals, the *'Shitamachi* occupational therapist pro bono team OCCULABO,' to provide occupational activities through which everyone in the community can support each other to live happily and pleasurably through participation in social activities and interaction with other residents. These activities include:

- Organizing meetings to discuss systems and activities needed in the community
- Advice about dementia
- Advice about childrearing
- Advice about daily living
- Medical advice
- Community interaction
- Children's cafeteria (described below)
- Provision of venues for residents' activities
- Literacy programs

The project is inclusive of all age groups, from babies to elderly people, and is based on the idea that everyone in the community is a member of one family. With the support from occupational therapists joining in the group, we hope that the people in the community will establish the social ties that will enable them to tackle their issues as one team.

The aims of OCCULABO are to support the everyday life (occupation) of community residents by taking advantage of a wide variety of specializations by using a multidisciplinary approach based in occupational and physical therapies, nursing and care, and in particular, to build positive intergenerational connections between children and elderly people. While OCCULABO aims to expand its activities and to undertake commissioned programs by registering with the public administration as a *pro bono* team, in order to carry out the activities for *all* people, Hajime and the staff consider their activities as '*sukedachi*' or voluntary support for the broader population, instead of using terms such as 'care' or 'nursing'. Hajime considers it necessary to establish an independent system, initially supported by public funds, to continue training people and developing their capacity to take initiative by organizing and demonstrating actual activities for which volunteers are needed. Some detailed examples are listed below. (Without registration, no organization or group can be commissioned from official entities, councils or authorities in Japan.)

Examples of 'sukedachi' activities

- *'Shitamachi'* Life Café [2]
  This is OCCULABO's main activity, which is organized six times a year. *Shitamachi* Life Cafés are organized to offer group counseling (advice sessions). After each session, individual counseling is provided if desired – participants living in the same community may prefer not to discuss certain issues in groups. Additional counseling is also available by e-mails and over the phone as time permits. Currently, 5-8 persons participate in each event although there are spaces for 20 persons. The occupational therapists' involvement has been increased: one example is the Minkuru café, as described below. Hajime has invited other occupational therapists to join in these activities as *probono* volunteers.

- The Minkuru Café

  The Minkuru Café is a children's cafeteria, providing cooked food for children in poverty, catering for 50 at one time, although more can come in a different sitting. Its work involves promoting the bringing of children into the workplace. Parents need to work for their living, but nursery schools are already full and cannot accept any more children. A solution which enables parents to continue earning and look after their children is to allow parents to bring their children to their workplaces and access advice about childcare, including matching parents with volunteer baby sitters (a qualification is not required), and nursing care;

- Occupational therapists are also involved in giving advice and support for outings and travel for persons with disabilities and elderly people, and support for homeless people. There are plans to provide them with information and make connections for them with health services, in addition to job matching and support for re-employment, including vocational training.

Who are these activities targeting?

- Everyone: although the main persons targeted by OCCULABO are homeless people, persons with disabilities and families in poverty, it has the objective of supporting the social participation of minorities and of promoting the value of interaction between minority and majority groups. The Japanese newspaper Asahi Shimbun reported in 2015 that families with an annual income of less than 1,220 thousand yen (12,200 USD) are considered to be in poverty in Japan; the poverty rate for families with children under 18 years old was 16.3% in 2012.
- Babies and elderly people: the targeted persons include not only the service users (clients) themselves but also their families such as the parents of babies, their friends or other members of the community, including the staff of public administration organizations and business enterprises with whom they interact;
- Anyone with or without mental, developmental or physical disabilities, social welfare benefits recipients, homeless people or persons living in poverty (for example, single-mother households).

How to implement 'sukedachi'

Sukedachi activities are organized six times a year, either at a café or a similar facility. They take the form of a seminar where participants can gain some ideas about daily living through dialogue. Participants are charged 100 – 3,000 yen ($1 - 30 USD at the time of writing), a rate which is not a burden to most families, depending on the content of the activity and the cost of the facility used, including the cost of a drink. Other activities promote the community to become one 'family' and encourage the residents to support each other. It is expected that participants will gain some knowledge through these activities and learn to support others in the town through friendly community relations and contributing their skills based around the needs people have for help.

Participants are given group counselling about occupation (concerning living, working and environment) and quality of life by applying occupational assessments: ensuring mothers' quality of life, counselling for fathers on supporting children and maintaining a suitable work-life balance. (See also http://shitamachioccupati.wix. com/shitamachi-occulabo)

Future plans

As well as the activities already taking place, as described above, Hajime plans to organize the following activities in the future:

- Creating a baseball team with the people with higher brain dysfunction who wish to play games again, by making tools and drawing rules designated to their conditions;
- Activities to raise social sensitivity towards persons with disabilities: conducting research at a shopping mall as to whether people notice persons with disabilities (some disabilities are visible while the others are invisible) and make consideration on the circumstances. The purpose of the research is to provide a number of opportunities for many people to experience diversity as an actual encounter, which may create an awareness.
- Organizing a children's cafeteria to provide support for families in poverty, as well as to provide a venue for community residents without connections and interactions with other residents. The cafeteria is not only a venue where people cook and eat together but also to have multigenerational communication. The cafeteria would provide some games and a supplementary education for children who are not able to go to private tutoring schools (it is comm\on in Japan to go to private tutoring schools in addition to normal schools under the educational curriculum).

Conclusion

Townsend (2009) identified ten key enablement skills in occupational therapy: adapt, advocate, coach, collaborate, consult, coordinate, design/build, educate, engage and specialize. If occupational therapists were only to apply these key therapy skills in hospitals it would be difficult to understand broader issues about clients' social environment, works and roles, and systems surrounding them. Occupational therapists need to do more than focus on disabilities and engage with political and public administrations to address problems which lie deep in social systems. Townsend's ten key enablement skills not only apply to occupational therapists' work in hospitals, but imply becoming active in wider society where people's social bonds and their minds are subjugated to a prioritized value of efficiency. Through an application of their skills and strengths in social intervention occupational therapists can make a vital social contribution to enabling everyone to have a happier life quality.

Although Japan is recognized as an economically developed country, not everyone enjoys a wealthy lifestyle; on the contrary, one in every six persons lives in relative poverty and social inequity. As a result, the doors for the future of children living under these conditions are barred. Thus, Hajime aims to contribute to society through community based occupational therapy interventions that bring occupational fairness to communities, and hopes to tackle the social aspects of functional disorders such as lack of information or diluted human bonds.

Notes

1   Small Multi-care Facility 'Otagaisan' by Aoicare Co., Ltd. (www.aoicare.com)
     Small Multi-care Facility 'Kizuna' by CANNUS Group (http://nurse.jp/)
     Small Multi-care Facility 'Yurari Club' by Life Help Service Co., Ltd. (http://l-helpservice.com/company.html)
2   'Minkuru' Café: (http://www.mincle-produce.net/

References

Cabinet Office of Japan (2013) *FY2013 Young Core Leaders of Civil Society Groups Development Program*, 271

Daigo, K. (2015) That's why occupational therapist, let's do the social contribution activity. *Clinical occupational therapy*, 12, 1, 20-25

Kingston, J. (2011) *Contemporary Japan: History, politics and social change since the 1980s.* Chichester:Wiley

Mugiwara, H (2013) Influence of pre-after young period's personality formation, from the view of under three-year-old day nursery: No.1 From theory of Bowlby's attachment and Erikson's Life cycle; *Bulletin of Shukutoku University Junior College*, 52, 43-60

Sawamura, K. (2013) Relationship between parents' attachment to their child and the child's mood states and psychosomatic states in adolescence. *Japan Society of Health Evaluation and Promotion*, 40, 2, 253-258

Sugawara, M. (1997) Parental mental health and the child personality development: A review on maternal depression; *The Japanese Journal of Personality*, 5, 38-55

Townsend, E. (2009) *The World at Our Feet: Walking the global talk of collaborative, experience-based practices*, December

Yamaguchi, A. (2015) Influences of quality of life on health and well-being. *Social Indicators Research*, 123, 1, 77-102

Index

Note: Page locators in *italic* refer to figures or photographs.